D0443576

ECON OMIC
INEQUALITY

THE AMERICAN DREAM UNDER SIEGE

CORAL CELESTE FRAZER

TWENTY-FIRST CENTURY BOOKS / MINNEAPOLIS

To Michael and Oren

Text copyright © 2018 by Lerner Publishing Group, Inc.

All rights reserved. International copyright secured. No part of this book may be reproduced, stored in a retrieval system, or transmitted in any form or by any means— electronic, mechanical, photocopying, recording, or otherwise—without the prior written permission of Lerner Publishing Group, Inc., except for the inclusion of brief quotations in an acknowledged review.

Twenty-First Century Books
A division of Lerner Publishing Group, Inc.
241 First Avenue North
Minneapolis, MN 55401 USA

For reading levels and more information, look up this title at www.lernerbooks.com.

Main body text set in Adobe Garamond Pro 11/15.
Typeface provided by Adobe Systems.

Library of Congress Cataloging-in-Publication Data

Names: Frazer, Coral Celeste, author.
Title: Economic inequality : the American dream under siege / Coral Celeste Frazer.
Description: Minneapolis : Twenty-First Century Books, [2018] | Audience: Age: 13–18. | Audience: Grade 9 to 12. | Includes bibliographical references and index.
Identifiers: LCCN 2017032058| ISBN 9781512431070 (lb) | ISBN 9781512498868 (eb pdf)
Subjects: LCSH: Income distribution—United States—Juvenile literature. | United States—Economic conditions—Juvenile literature. | United States—Economic policy—Juvenile literature.
Classification: LCC HC110.I5 F738 2018 | DDC 339.2/20973—dc23

LC record available at https://lccn.loc.gov/2017032058

Manufactured in the United States of America
1-41668-23517-10/3/2017

CONTENTS

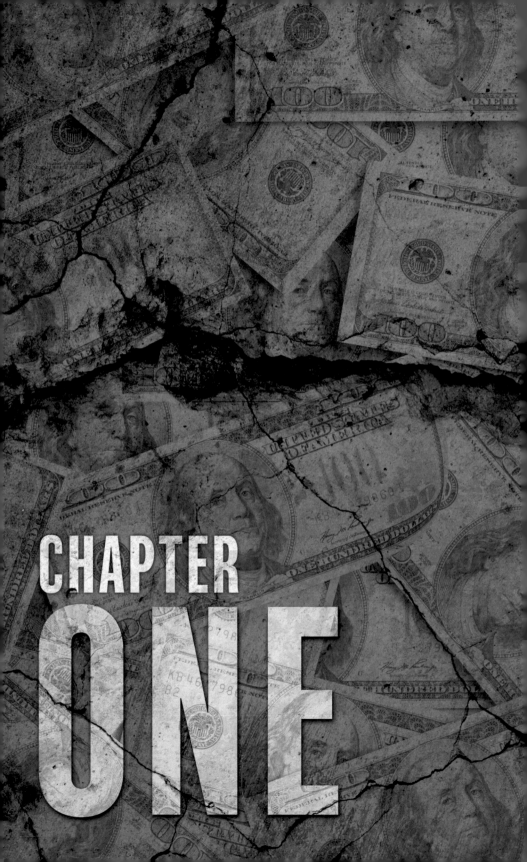

CHAPTER
ONE

THE RISE AND FALL AND RISE OF AMERICAN INEQUALITY

Imagine a giant balancing scale. One side holds all the money and wealth of the four richest Americans in 2016: Bill Gates of Microsoft ($81 billion); Jeff Bezos of Amazon.com ($67 billion); Warren Buffett of the business conglomerate Berkshire Hathaway ($65.5 billion); and Mark Zuckerberg, founder of Facebook ($55.5 billion). Their combined total wealth in 2016 was $269 billion.

Bill Gates, founder of Microsoft, speaks at a conference in China in 2017. One of the richest people on Earth, Gates had $86 billion in wealth that year.

Now imagine loading the other side of the scale with the wealth of enough Americans to balance the scale on both sides. To balance that $269 billion owned by just *four* men on the one side, you'd need to pile up the combined wealth of the poorest *128 million* Americans on the other side. This imbalance—the enormous gap between rich and poor—perfectly illustrates economic inequality in the United States.

It is easy to think about the gap between the rich and the poor as unchangeable—something that has always been there, will always be there, and isn't worth worrying too much about. But economic inequality matters. When a very few people are rich and a great number of people are poor, humans suffer and so does the economy. Economic growth (an increase in the amount of business activity and goods produced over time) slows, and the economy can take sudden downturns. When that happens, businesses fail, unemployment rises, more people fall into poverty, and some people fall deeply into debt.

In the early twenty-first century in the United States, the gap between rich and poor is large and it's getting larger. But that gap is not unchangeable. Through nearly 250 years of American history, economic inequality has risen and then fallen and then risen again. And during those rises and falls, some Americans have prospered while many others have suffered.

THE COLONIES AND THE EARLY REPUBLIC

During the American Revolution (1775–1783), when American colonists fought for independence from Great Britain, about 20 percent of the colonial population were enslaved African Americans. They had no legal rights and could not own land or other property. By law they were property—they belonged to their masters, who could buy or sell them. They had no wealth of their own.

White American colonists had plenty of land to farm. With natural resources (such as timber, fish, and animal skins) to harvest and sell, many white colonists prospered. And income in colonial America was more equally distributed than in the twenty-first century. In 1774 about 8.5 percent of income went to the top 1 percent (the people who were richer than 99 percent of their fellow Americans), whereas in 2017, a whopping 20 percent of income goes to the top 1 percent.

Americans did less well economically from the mid-1770s to 1800, a period of turmoil and recovery from the destruction of war. The newly independent United States struggled to get on its feet. But by the early nineteenth century, the nation had established its political institutions, and prosperity was again on the rise. But so was economic inequality.

EARLY INDUSTRIALIZATION

The United States started the nineteenth century as an agrarian, or farming, society. Most American families grew their own food, made their own clothes and tools, and built their own houses. If a family needed something it couldn't make on its own, it usually bartered, or

In the early nineteenth century, most Americans worked for themselves, as farmers or craftspeople. Later in the century, with the rise of factories and big business, more Americans worked for employers.

traded, for it. A farm family might swap a barrel of apples for a tool made by a blacksmith, for example.

Over the first half of the nineteenth century, the nation made a gradual transition to a more cash-based and market-driven economy. Farmers and craftspeople started to produce crops and other goods to sell rather than to use for themselves or barter with their neighbors. This period also saw the rise of big cities and of the first US factories. Historians refer to the rise of factory production as the Industrial Revolution. Over time, consumers bought more and more goods produced in large factories rather than making them at home or in small workshops. More Americans became wage laborers. Rather than working for themselves, they worked for an employer, who paid them a set wage. These changes increased economic inequality in the United States. Factory owners, merchants, and other businesspeople made a lot of money. Wage laborers barely got by, and enslaved peoples worked for no pay at all. The gap between the rich and poor increased.

THE GILDED AGE

By the late 1870s, industrialization was in full swing. Production of steel and iron—to make trains, railroad ties, bridges, office buildings, and other vehicles and structures—skyrocketed. Railroads crisscrossed the nation, transporting valuable natural resources such as timber, oil, gold, and silver from the West to the industrial cities of the Northeast. The United States was rushing headlong into a period of great wealth—and stark inequality.

This period, known as the Gilded Age, gave birth to the fortunes of the richest Americans of all time: John D. Rockefeller (1839–1937) and Andrew Carnegie (1835–1919). Critics called them robber barons because their business practices were ruthless and unethical. They paid their workers bare-bones wages and used their great wealth to influence politicians. Rockefeller made his fortune selling oil, which was in great demand to power machinery, including newly invented

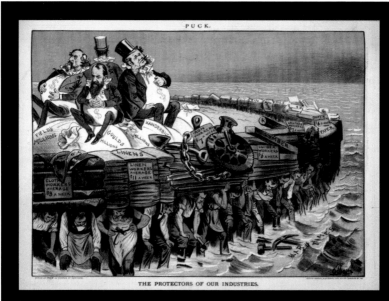

PUCK.

THE PROTECTORS OF OUR INDUSTRIES.

This cartoon from *Puck*, an American humor magazine, shows late nineteenth-century robber barons sitting on bags of money, on a dock loaded with oil, lumber, iron, and other industrial goods. Holding up the dock are struggling workers, whose bare-bones wages are also noted. They stand in a sea labeled "hard times."

automobiles. Carnegie made his wealth by manufacturing steel, used to make everything from household appliances to ships to tall buildings. In twenty-first-century dollars, the two men were worth about $336 billion (Rockefeller) and $309 billion (Carnegie).

In 1903 manufacturer Henry Ford founded the Ford Motor Company near Detroit, Michigan. At first, Ford workers built cars one at a time. It took about twelve worker hours to build one car. (A worker hour is the amount of work one person can do in one hour.) In 1913 Ford introduced the first rolling assembly line into his automobile factory. He broke down building a car into extremely small and simple tasks. Each worker was assigned one task. As each vehicle traveled along a conveyor belt, each worker performed his task, such as mounting a steering wheel or bolting on a fender. Cars rolled down them line one after another, and workers repeated their tasks over and over again, hour after hour. This system reduced the amount of time it took to build one car to just two and one-half worker hours. The system reduced manufacturing costs, so Ford could sell cars more cheaply than other carmakers. When cars had first been introduced, only the wealthy could afford to buy them. But as Ford reduced manufacturing costs and prices, cars became affordable for the average worker. Soon Ford's first assembly-line-produced cars, Model Ts, were commonplace, and Ford amassed a personal fortune worth $199 billion in 2017 dollars.

The idea of the assembly line spread quickly to other industries, and an era of mass production and mass consumption was born. Nationwide advertising campaigns touted newly invented household conveniences, including washing machines, radios, refrigerators, and vacuum cleaners. Stores and banks eagerly extended credit to consumers, lending them money so they could buy new products. Borrowers paid back the money, plus interest, over time.

THE ROARING TWENTIES

The 1920s—or the Roaring Twenties—was a decade of unprecedented prosperity. The nation's wealth doubled by the end of the decade. The growth of cities and new technology such as cars, movies, and radios contributed to the economic boom. But the soaring stock market was the biggest factor.

When people buy stock in a company, they are buying a share of ownership in that company. When the company makes money, the stockholder gets a share of the profits. If the company does poorly, the stockholder earns less or may lose money.

During the 1920s, borrowing money to buy stocks was easy. For each share of stock they wanted to buy, customers had to pay only 10 to 20 percent of the stock's price. Banks and stockbrokers (people who buy and sell stocks) loaned buyers the rest of the money.

If the company made money, the stockholder got a big payout and could easily pay back the loan, plus interest. Some investors became millionaires.

The prospect of making easy money drew more and more investors to buy stocks. With all that money pouring in, companies that sold shares to investors were flush with cash. They could pay high salaries to their executives, open new factories, and hire more employees. Because businesses were thriving, workers took home steady paychecks and bought new cars, houses, and consumer goods, either with cash or on credit. But the real gains fell into the hands of rich bankers, manufacturers, and business executives. In the 1920s, taxes on the wealthy were low, and the nation's top 1 percent earned 14.5 percent of the nation's total income. Things were even better for the richest of the rich. The nation's top 0.1 percent possessed about one-quarter of the country's wealth. Meanwhile, the bottom 90 percent held just 16 percent of the nation's wealth.

The prosperity of the 1920s extended only to white, male Americans. The Thirteenth Amendment to the US Constitution had ended slavery in the United States in 1865. But after that, states and cities passed laws barring black Americans from living in white neighborhoods, eating in restaurants with white people, and using the water fountains and restrooms that white people used. Buses and trains had separate areas for white and black passengers. Employers often refused to hire black workers except for the most low-status jobs, such as picking crops, shining shoes, and cleaning houses. Black workers received less pay than white workers, even when they did the same jobs. Black children and white children attended separate schools. Families of different races attended different churches, and whites and blacks rarely socialized or intermarried. School officials gave the most money and the best resources, such as new buildings, up-to-date books, and well-trained teachers, to white schools. They left black schools with run-down facilities, outdated books, and poorly trained teachers.

Traders buy and sell stocks on the New York Stock Exchange in the late 1920s. Stock prices soared during the decade, but in October 1929, prices plummeted and the US stock market crashed.

Besides inequality between blacks and whites, women suffered from unequal treatment. US women won the right to vote in 1920, but laws and customs kept most women from attending college, entering skilled professions, starting businesses, or accumulating wealth on their own. Society expected young women to quit their jobs when they got married and stay home to care for their husbands and children. Few women got rich on their own, although some prospered when they married wealthy men.

THE GREAT DEPRESSION

Throughout the 1920s, the value of stocks rose higher and higher. Many investors bought stocks at one price and quickly sold them for a big profit. In October 1929, everything changed. Stock prices, which had been rising steadily, all at once began to fall. Investors panicked, worried that prices would fall even more. Hoping to recoup at least some of their investment, thousands of stockholders sold their shares for a loss. The more investors sold, the more prices fell. In the course of four days, the stock market lost $30 billion in value—almost $400 billion in 2017 dollars. Many investors were wiped out completely. They couldn't pay back the banks that had lent them money to buy stocks. So the banks suffered enormous losses too.

Knowing that banks had lost a great deal of money, thousands of depositors rushed to withdraw their savings. They were afraid if they didn't hurry, the banks would go out of business and all their money would be lost. Banks do not keep all the money that customers deposit on hand, just sitting inside vaults. They lend much of it to businesses and individuals, so they can make money off the interest. During the 1920s, some banks had even invested depositors' money into the stock market—and had lost it when the market crashed. So when thousands of people wanted their money back at the same time, the banks couldn't keep up with the demand. Many banks ran out of cash and went broke.

WHAT IS WALL STREET?

Wall Street is the street in Manhattan (one of New York's City's five boroughs) where the New York Stock Exchange is located. Traders working for the New York Stock Exchange buy and sell stocks to and for big corporations and wealthy individuals. The exchange is the oldest stock market in the United States. Wall Street is also home to many large investment firms and banks. When people talk about Wall Street, they often mean the financial industry in general—big banks and investment firms, as well as the bankers and stockbrokers who work there.

The failure of the banks and the crash of the stock market brought on the economic hardship known as the Great Depression (1929–1942). With the loss of their savings and investments, Americans had much less money to buy goods. With fewer people buying products, many factories closed and laid off their workers. More unemployed Americans meant that even fewer people had money to buy consumer goods. More factories closed. Industrial production dropped to half of what it had been before the financial crisis, and many more workers lost their jobs. At the height of the Depression, in 1933, more than twelve million people, or one-quarter of working-age Americans, were unemployed.

Businesses that managed to stay afloat cut their workers' wages. Without jobs or with only low-paying jobs, many homeowners could not pay back the money they had borrowed to buy their houses. So the banks that had lent the money took ownership of the homes as a foreclosure. Families had to leave their homes, as did farmers who could not make their loan payments. After losing their homes and farms, thousands of Americans moved to homeless encampments. Others took to the road, hitching rides, sneaking onto trains, or traveling in broken-down cars to look for work elsewhere. Many US families did not have enough food to survive. Charities and state and federal agencies began to give out basic provisions. In cities, thousands of hungry people lined up for free meals every day.

In 1932 Americans elected Franklin Delano Roosevelt president. Roosevelt promised "a new deal" to help the poor and to get the economy growing again. A large part of the New Deal program was public works: the federal government hired millions of Americans to build schools, bridges, highways, dams, power plants, and government offices. The government also hired workers to care for public lands and artists and writers to document American life. It created programs to help farmers and extended low-interest loans to homeowners.

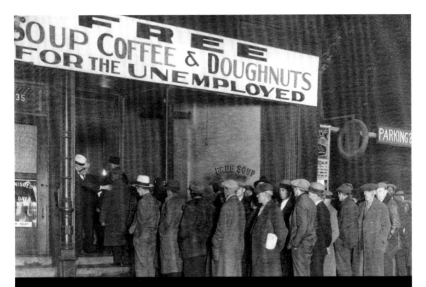

At the height of the Great Depression, about 25 percent of working-age Americans were unemployed. Hungry and desperate, many relied on food from charities and government relief programs.

Roosevelt also supported laws to make it easier for workers to form unions. These organizations of workers band together to negotiate with their employers for better wages, safer working conditions, paid time off, and other benefits. If the employers refuse to agree to what the workers ask for, the union might call a strike. During a strike, workers refuse to do their jobs until their demands are met and they can reach a compromise with management. By striking, unions try to bring businesses to a halt. Without workers to run their machines and operations, businesses can't produce and sell goods. They begin to lose money. The losses may pressure business leaders into agreeing to the workers' demands.

Many business owners and managers dislike unions because businesses can make more money by paying low wages. When organizers brought unions to the three major US auto manufacturers, General Motors, Chrysler, and Ford, in the late 1930s and early 1940s, management fiercely opposed them. Sometimes bosses hired thugs to

UNION BUSTING ◄-------------------------

Henry Ford (*right*) was strongly opposed to unions. He hired men to threaten workers who tried to distribute union literature at his factories. For example, on May 26, 1937, in an incident dubbed the Battle of the Overpass, Ford security workers violently attacked United Automobile Workers (UAW) organizers at a Ford plant near Detroit. The attackers not only punched and kicked the organizers, but they also tried to rip film out of the photographers' cameras and pull notebooks from journalists' hands so they couldn't report on the violence. All the same, photos of the attack made it into newspapers around the country. As a result, Americans threw their support behind the UAW, and Ford was unionized in 1941.

physically attack union organizers and striking workers, and hired scabs (nonunion workers) to do their jobs. But with government backing, unions persisted. Their negotiations with bosses paid off in improved wages and working conditions.

THE GREAT PROSPERITY

New Deal programs helped many Americans get back on their feet. But the Depression truly ended only after the United States entered World War II (1939–1945) in 1941. The fighting had begun in Europe in 1939, and at first, the United States stayed out of the war. But on December 7, 1941, Japan bombed a US naval base at Pearl Harbor, Hawaii. The next day, the United States declared war on Japan and its allies, Germany and Italy.

The war effort revved up the US economy almost overnight. Factories that had closed during the Depression reopened, many of them converting from making civilian goods to making military supplies. During the war, US manufacturing created seventeen million new jobs. Millions of men joined the US armed forces, leaving factories, offices, farms, and shipyards with a shortage of workers. To keep these businesses running, many women took jobs that had previously been held only by men. They built tanks and bombers, operated machinery, drove trucks, and did other strenuous work. And businesses that had previously refused to hire Americans of color began to offer them jobs because they were desperate for workers. Suddenly the economy was booming again.

Manufacturing remained strong after the end of World War II. With high employment rates, consumers had money to spend, and factories churned out consumer goods such as cars, refrigerators, and television sets. The postwar period (1945–early 1970s) was a time of great prosperity. A federal law, the Servicemen's Readjustment Act of

This 1950s advertising illustration depicts American prosperity in the years following World War II. As the economy boomed, many middle-class Americans bought new cars and spacious suburban homes.

1944, known as the GI Bill, gave returning soldiers (nicknamed GIs) unemployment benefits if they could not find jobs. GIs could also get money for college or trade school and low-interest loans to start businesses or buy homes. As a result, the US middle class swelled after World War II. The federal government also imposed high tax rates on businesses and the rich. The more they prospered, the more money they had to pay to the US Treasury (a federal agency that oversees government income, spending, borrowing, and other finances). All this tax money helped pay for government programs, including the military, public education, roads and bridges, and scientific research. College enrollment soared.

Due to advances in technology and a better-educated workforce, productivity rose—workers were producing more per hour worked. This meant more profits for companies. With government policies that bolstered the strength of unions, workers were able to demand a share of those profits as higher wages. Workers, top management, and investors all prospered. However, for workers, the good times didn't last.

UNION BLUES

After about three decades of prosperity, economic inequality was once again on the rise in the United States. Starting in the late 1970s, productivity growth slowed for a time. It soon picked back up, but wages did not rise along with it. In the 1980s, strong productivity resulted in strong profits. But the profits went to top management, company owners, and stockholders. Workers did not see a significant rise in pay.

Why not? Mainly, it was because US unions were losing strength. In 1960, 24 percent of the American workforce was employed in manufacturing. And the manufacturing sector had the strongest unions, such as the United Automobile Workers and the United Steelworkers. But in the last decades of the twentieth century, the US

Electrical workers in New Jersey strike for higher wages in 1946. US unions were large and strong in the 1940s, 1950s, and 1960s. But in the 1970s, when US manufacturing started to shrink, union membership declined as well.

manufacturing sector began to shrink. Fewer manufacturing jobs meant fewer workers who could benefit from unions.

Why did manufacturing shrink? To save money on labor costs, in the late 1970s, US companies began moving manufacturing plants to other countries, a trend called overseas outsourcing. People in poor countries will work for much less money than American workers will accept. That's partly because housing and food cost less in poor nations, so workers don't need as much income. And many people in poor nations are desperate for work. They will accept extremely low wages because any job is better than no job. In the twenty-first century, for example, factory workers in China and Mexico earn less than four dollars an hour, while US factory workers make between ten and twenty dollars an hour. By 1990, 3 percent of the world's goods by value were produced in China. By 2015 that number was nearly 25 percent. And almost half of all goods were produced in Southeast Asia.

The decline of US manufacturing came especially fast in the early twenty-first century, with five million manufacturing jobs lost between 2000 and 2016. The reasons for the decline included both outsourcing and automation (robots and other machines taking over for human workers). By 2016 only 8 percent of the US workforce was employed in manufacturing. The loss has been painful for many American communities, especially since for many decades, manufacturing provided some of the best-paid jobs for people without a college degree.

As the US manufacturing sector has shrunk, the US service sector has grown. The service sector includes jobs in stores, restaurants, banks, hotels, schools, hospitals, government agencies, media companies, and social service organizations. The service sector has only a few unions. Most service sector workers do not receive the high pay and good benefits that unionized workers enjoy.

OUTSOURCED AND AUTOMATED

Manufacturing jobs are not the only victims of outsourcing. By telephone, web chat, and e-mail, customer service reps and other employees can work from anywhere in the world. Many companies have set up customer service call centers in India. In this poor nation with almost fifty million unemployed people, workers will accept much lower pay than American workers will. Computer programmers are in high demand, and they too can work from anywhere in the world. So can pharmacy technicians, medical transcriptionists, and bookkeepers. Increasingly, companies are hiring foreign workers to do these jobs from their home countries.

Jobs are also being lost to automation, with robots, computers, and

English-speaking customer service reps take phone calls from Americans at a call center in Bangalore, India. Overseas call centers save businesses a lot of money, because in poor nations such as India, workers are paid much lower wages than Americans are.

other smart machines doing tasks humans once performed. This trend is not new. Machines have been replacing human labor since the dawn of industrialization. For instance, women once made their family's clothing by hand at home. But during the Industrial Revolution, textile manufacturing changed radically. With new mechanical gins, spinning machines, and looms, textile production moved out of the home and into large factories.

In the twenty-first century, computers and smart technology are accelerating the trend toward automation. The key is routinization— the more predictable a task is, the more easily a computer can be programmed to do it. Already, online appointment-booking systems are replacing receptionists. Camera surveillance is replacing security guards, and self-checkout kiosks and online shopping have replaced cashiers. Telemarketers have lost their jobs to robocalls.

For much of the twentieth century, human workers built cars as they rolled down assembly lines. In the twenty-first century, robots do most of the work. Here robots assemble Jeep Grand Cherokees at a factory in Detroit, Michigan.

Self-driving vehicles are becoming a reality in the United States and western Europe, and soon taxi and delivery drivers may be replaced too. In some cases, computers can perform even highly skilled jobs. For instance, computers can examine X-rays and CT scans for signs of cancer, and sometimes they can do so more accurately than experienced radiologists. The trend of automation is likely to continue. A 2013 study by Carl Benedikt Frey and Michael A. Osborne of Oxford University estimated that 47 percent of American jobs had the potential of being done by machines.

With machines taking over so many routine, semiskilled jobs, the global job market is becoming polarized. On one end are low-skill, low-paying jobs such as cleaning and food preparation. On the other are high-skill, high-paying jobs in fields such as software development, pharmacy, and medicine. The jobs being lost are the ones in between: middle-class jobs (in office work, manufacturing, and social work, for instance) that pay middle-of-the-road wages.

IMMIGRATION

Immigration also plays a role in the American job market, although a much lesser role than outsourcing and automation. Immigrants often benefit the US economy. They bring new skills and entrepreneurship. Many immigrants are leaders in the booming US tech industry, for instance. Immigrants also take jobs in labor-scarce regions or accept difficult, low-paying jobs that American-born workers are reluctant to do, such as harvesting crops by hand, cleaning hotel rooms, and working in meat-processing plants. However, critics of immigration note that when foreign workers enter the job market in large numbers, they compete with US-born workers for jobs. The newcomers, eager to get a foothold in the United States, are often willing to work for lower wages than native-born workers will accept. So immigrants land jobs that some argue should go to native-born Americans.

With trends such as outsourcing, automation, and tax policies that favor the rich, the Great Prosperity is over. Young Americans entering the workforce enter a very different environment than what their parents and grandparents experienced decades earlier. The United States has always been a nation of haves and have-nots, but in the twenty-first century, the gap between those two extremes is greater than ever before.

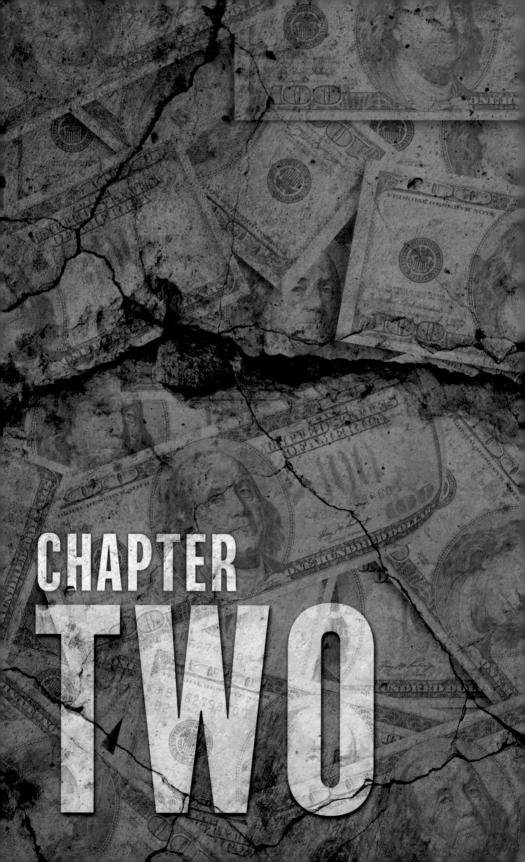

CHAPTER
TWO

HOW UNEQUAL ARE WE?

Suppose you earn $7,500 this year by working after-school and summer jobs. It would be nice to put that money in the bank. But even with that income, you might not feel so wealthy if you owed $10,000 to an uncle who had loaned you money to buy a car. If you paid him the $7,500, you'd be back to zero—and you'd still owe $2,500. The example shows that income and wealth are not the same thing.

People earn income in different ways. Some work after school or full-time. Others invest their money in businesses and get a share of the profits if these businesses make money.

A person's income includes the total amount of money earned through work and investments over the course of a year. Wealth is usually measured at the household or family level. A family's wealth is calculated by adding the value of its assets—money and property—and subtracting the value of its debts—the amount of money the family owes. Wealth is also called net worth.

Politicians and journalists sometimes discuss income and wealth as averages. For instance, in 2014 the average household income in the United States was $73,298. But the word *average* is not precise because it can refer to one of two things: the mean value of a group of numbers or the median value of a group of numbers. The mean value of household income in the United States is calculated by adding all the income earned by all US households and then dividing that number by the number of households. The median value is the income in the middle of that same list of household incomes. The household with the median income would earn more than half of the earners and less than the other half.

In the United States, a lot of wealth is concentrated in the hands of relatively few people. For example, the top 1 percent of Americans takes in nearly one-quarter of the income earned in the nation each year.

Mean and median numbers are often very far apart and can be misleading. For instance, the mean wealth (income divided by households) of adults in the United States is roughly $275,000. That sounds good, right? But the median wealth (midway marker) of US adults is only about $39,000. How can this be? Say you calculated the mean wealth of eleven people eating in a restaurant on a certain night—and one of them was Bill Gates, the richest man in the world. To find the mean, you'd add all the net wealth of those diners and divide by eleven. Here's how the equation might look (remember that net wealth is a number based on assets minus debt):

DINER	NET WORTH (IN DOLLARS IN 2016)
Bill Gates	81,000,000,000
Ms. A	500,000
Mr. B	150,000
Ms. C	100,000
Mr. D	95,000
Ms. E	70,000
Mr. F	65,000
Ms. G	40,000
Mr. H	6,000
Ms. I	100
Mr. J	0
TOTAL	81,001,026,100

The mean wealth of this group is about $7.4 billion. Yet the person with the median wealth on this list is Ms. E, with only $70,000. Five people on the list have more wealth than she does, and five people have less. Using $70,000 for the average (or median) wealth of the group gives a much more accurate picture than using the mean wealth. So, when talking about economic inequality, it is most useful to talk about medians rather than means.

THE HAVES, THE HAVE-NOTS, AND THE HAVE LOTS

In the United States, a lot of wealth is concentrated in the hands of relatively few people. For example, the top 1 percent of Americans takes in nearly one-quarter of the income earned in the nation each year.

They possess more than one-third of the wealth in the nation. And there is a surprising amount of inequality even *within* the top 1 percent. The richest members of the 1 percent are corporate executives, tech wizards, and investment managers who rake in millions of dollars each year. But at the bottom of the 1 percent are well-paid doctors, lawyers, and other professionals making a comparatively modest $400,000 a year.

Why are the numbers so lopsided? Why do so many people have so little wealth while so much wealth is in the hands of so few? Part of the reason is debt. About half of Americans owe at least as much as they own, giving them a net worth of zero. Although some of these people own their own homes and have some savings and investments in stocks, the amount of money they owe on their mortgages (home loans), car and school loans, credit cards, and other bills is even greater.

THE WALTON FAMILY ←----------------------

Sam Walton (*right*) and his brother, James, opened the first Wal-Mart store in Rogers, Arkansas, in 1962. Wal-Mart Stores Inc. has since grown to become the world's largest retailer, with $482 billion in annual sales. The seven heirs to the Wal-Mart fortune (the brothers' children and grandchildren) are the richest family in the United States and the second-richest family in the world (after the royal family of Saudi Arabia). Together, they own about half of the company stock, putting their net worth at about $130 billion. An article on the Economic Policy Institute website stated that in 2010, the heirs had as much wealth as the poorest 48.8 million families in the United States combined.

Another measure of inequality in society is called the Gini index. On this scale, 0 indicates total equality—everyone earns the same income (wages) or has the same amount of wealth (assets minus debt). On the same scale, 100 equals perfect inequality—a single person has all the income or all the wealth and everyone else has nothing. The higher the score on the Gini index, the more unequal a society is. The United States has a Gini score of 41. Compared to most industrialized nations, that's pretty high. Ukraine, Slovenia, and Norway have the lowest levels of inequality, with Gini scores in the mid-20s. South Africa, Haiti, and Namibia are the most unequal, with scores in the low 60s.

DEMOGRAPHICS

Who are the fortunate Americans at the top end of the economic ladder? Geographically, the wealthy tend to cluster around big cities, especially those where specific business sectors are based. These places and specific sectors include New York City, financial industry; Washington, DC, federal government; the San Francisco Bay Area, the computer industry; and Los Angeles, the TV and film industry. In contrast, far fewer wealthy people live in southeastern states, such as Alabama, Kentucky, Mississippi, and Tennessee, because these states lack rich industries comparable to Wall Street or Silicon Valley (a nickname for the cities near San Francisco where many tech businesses are headquartered). For example, in Silicon Valley, 16 percent of households are in the top 5 percent. In Louisville, Kentucky, only 3.5 percent of households are in the top 5 percent.

The wealthiest Americans are also overwhelmingly (96 percent) white. White families make up 63 percent of the US population but hold 90 percent of the nation's wealth. The net worth of the median white family in the United States is $134,000, while the median black family has a net worth of only $11,000 and the median Hispanic family of only $14,000. Roughly one-quarter of Hispanic and black

MEDIAN US FAMILY WEALTH BY RACE, 2013*

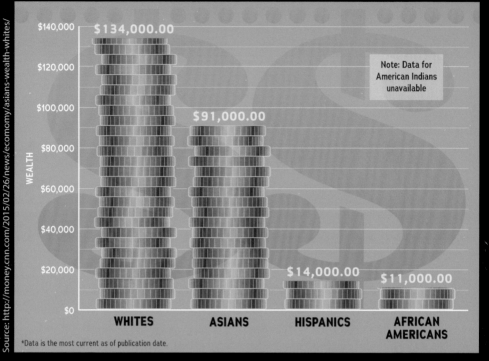

Source: http://money.cnn.com/2015/02/26/news/ecomomy/asians-wealth-whites/

WEALTH

$140,000 — $134,000.00

$120,000

$100,000

$80,000 — $91,000.00

$60,000

$40,000

$20,000 — $14,000.00 — $11,000.00

$0

WHITES   **ASIANS**   **HISPANICS**   **AFRICAN AMERICANS**

Note: Data for American Indians unavailable

*Data is the most current as of publication date.

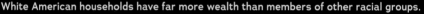

White American households have far more wealth than members of other racial groups.

families live in poverty. More than 28 percent of American Indians live in poverty. (According to US government guidelines, a family of four living on less than $24,300 a year is said to be living in poverty.) By contrast, about 10 percent of white families live in poverty.

What accounts for these differences? Racial inequality is a reality at every level of American society. Because of the nation's long, persistent history of racism, white Americans are much more likely than blacks, Hispanics, or American Indians to be hired for jobs, receive raises, go to top colleges, receive business and mortgage loans, and be welcomed into neighborhoods with good schools. This success translates into higher earnings.

It's harder to compare net worth in the United States by gender. This is because economists generally measure wealth by household or family rather than by individual. More than 50 percent of households in the United States consist of a man and woman living together, often with children. When economists calculate wealth, they do it for the family unit—not for individual spouses. But when economists break down statistics along gender lines, the data show that men have much more wealth than women. The inequality is easier to measure by looking at income. While women make up 47 percent of the US workforce, they make up only about 17 percent of the top 1 percent of income earners.

On average, women earn about seventy-nine cents for every dollar men earn. This gap stems from a combination of laws and social customs. In the early years of the United States, colleges were for men only. That began to change in the late nineteenth century, when a few women's colleges opened in the eastern United States. In the twentieth century, laws changed and more colleges accepted women, so more women attended college and earned degrees. Some did not pursue careers outside the home afterward. Others chose careers, but the only occupations that were open to women were caregiving professions such as nursing, teaching, counseling, and social work—and these were low-paying fields. For much of the twentieth century, high-paying fields such as manufacturing, medicine, computer programming, banking, and

OPRAH WINFREY ◄-----------------------------------

Oprah Winfrey is the richest black person in the United States. Famous for her long-running daytime talk show and book club, Winfrey also owns her own cable TV network (OWN), acts in movies, appears on the CBS news show *60 Minutes*, and owns 10 percent of the Weight Watchers weight-loss company. Her current net worth is about $3.1 billion. Many white American men are much richer than Winfrey. On the list of the richest people in the United States, she is number 214.

MEDIAN ANNUAL EARNINGS FOR FULL-TIME US WORKERS, BY GENDER AND RACE, 2013*

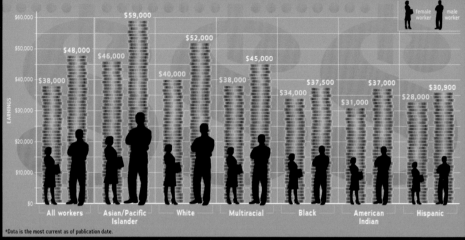

*Data is the most current as of publication date.

Source: http://statusofwomendata.org/explore-the-data/employment-and-earnings/emloyment-and-earnings/#MedianAnnualEarnings

Asian and white workers make more money than those in other racial groups. Within every racial group, men earn more money than women.

engineering were off-limits to women. Many colleges would not allow women to train in these professions. Firms would not hire women for these jobs, even if they had the proper training.

The women's movement of the 1960s and 1970s helped break down these barriers. Professional schools and associations opened their doors to women, and many women trained for high-paying jobs. In the twenty-first century, American women are more likely than American men to receive a bachelor's degree during their twenties. Women and men are equally likely to go to graduate school, and many women are moving into high-paying fields. But even in these fields, women don't earn as much as men. For example, in 2015 female doctors and surgeons had a median weekly income of $1,246, while the median for their male counterparts was $2,002 a week. One explanation for the pay differences is that women sometimes take time off work or reduce their work hours when they have children. Fewer work hours translates into less income. Sexism also plays a big part. Society, in general, perceives women as less confident, less capable, and less deserving of high wages than men. If a woman is not assertive on the job, her male coworkers might question her leadership abilities. But if she shows too much confidence, her male coworkers might criticize her for being pushy. Either way, a male boss might pass her over for a raise or promotion. Data show that professional women are not only paid less than male counterparts but are also less likely to be promoted to high management positions. And few women hold the very top positions.

MONEY MAKES MONEY

Want to get rich? If you already have money, that's not hard to do. French economist Thomas Piketty made headlines in 2013 by pointing out how much richer the rich have been getting since the late twentieth century. Piketty says the self-perpetuating nature of wealth makes this possible. So if you're rich, you and the generations that come after you will most likely remain rich.

If you have a large amount of money and you want it to grow, all you have to do is invest it. Two of the most common types of investments are stocks and bonds. Buying stocks means buying a share of a company. When the company makes money, the stockholders get a portion of the profits. Buying bonds involves lending money to a business or a government for a period of time. The buyer pays a certain amount for the bond. After an agreed-upon time (such as a year), the business or government pays the buyer back, with interest. Most wealthy people invest their money in many different stocks and bonds. Even if an individual investment loses money, portfolios (group of investments) usually make money overall. So investing generally leads to more wealth.

About one-third of the world's billionaires (there are 1,810 of them) inherited their fortunes. They did not work for them. And they continue to amass wealth just by investing. When they die, they will likely pass their wealth onto their children, who also won't have to work. They can accumulate even more wealth by investing in new or existing businesses.

But many rich people *do* work. After all, two-thirds of the world's billionaires did not inherit their money. They earned it by their own efforts. Many of them made their fortunes by founding or leading global corporations. Executives have always been paid well. In 1973 a chief executive officer (CEO) generally made about 73 times as much as the typical company worker. Pay for top executives skyrocketed starting in the 1980s. By 2015 the CEOs of the richest five hundred companies in the United States made 340 times as much as the typical worker. On average, each CEO earned about $12.4 million a year. Adding to their wealth, most top executives are paid in stocks as well as wages. When the stocks increase in value, the executives make money without doing any work.

Most ordinary workers, on the other hand, earn only wages. And while the wages of top executives have risen dramatically, the wages of average workers have not grown at all over the past forty or fifty years. It looks as if wages have grown. For instance, in 1970 the minimum wage (the lowest amount employers are legally allowed to pay workers) was $1.60 an hour. In 2014 the minimum wage was $7.25 an hour. That's an increase of 353 percent. But $7.25 an hour didn't buy as much in 2014 as $1.60 an hour did in 1970. That's because the cost of food, housing, and everything else increased by a greater percentage

BONUS BONANZA

Wall Street firms are famous for handing out big bonuses to their employees at year's end. For experienced traders, multimillion-dollar bonuses are common. In 2014 Wall Street banks gave out $28.5 billion in bonuses to 167,800 employees. That's twice as much money in bonuses as all minimum wage workers in the nation (combined) earned that year.

TYPICAL YEARLY EARNINGS, 1978* AND 2010**

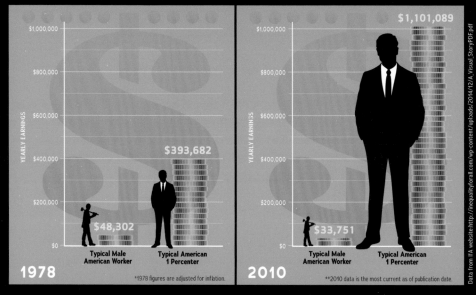

In 1978 the typical American 1 percenter earned about eight times more than the typical male American worker. By 2010 the 1 percenter earned more than thirty-two times as much.

than wages did. For instance, the cost of college tuition increased by 994 percent between 1970 and 2014. The cost of housing increased 917 percent in that period. The cost of household goods increased 482 percent. The rising price of goods and services (economic activity such as Internet banking, medical care, and car repair) is called inflation.

To compare wages from one period to another, economists must adjust for inflation. In 1970 bank tellers earned about $4,680 a year. When adjusted for inflation, this equals about $26,000 in 2010 dollars. Compare this to what bank tellers earned in 2010: $24,000 a year. This comparison shows that the pay for bank tellers has decreased over forty years. (And besides the pay decrease, bank tellers are increasingly losing their jobs to automation.) The same is true for many other jobs. Overall, wages for ordinary workers have stagnated since the 1970s.

THE POVERTY LINE

According to the Urban Institute, which studies social and economic policy, almost 40 percent of all American children will be poor for at least one year before they turn eighteen. The US government uses a formula based on the cost of food to define the poverty line. In 2016 the federal poverty line was $24,300 a year for a family of four and $11,880 for an individual. Families and individuals who earned less than this are officially considered poor, even though people who make more may also struggle to make ends meet.

Poverty and economic inequality are related. But they are not quite the same. Inequality means that goods and income are distributed unequally, so that some people get more than others. Poverty means a person or a family does not have enough money to meet the cost of basic daily needs, such as housing, transportation, and food. Rising inequality often accompanies increased poverty. This is true in the United States, where 15 percent of people live in poverty.

While the national poverty rate is 15 percent, an estimated 21 percent of American children are poor. That's because it takes much more money to support a family than to support one adult. An adult living alone must support only himself or herself. If the person works full-time for the federal minimum wage or more, he or she lives above the poverty line. If that same worker must support one or more nonworking children, the family will fall below the poverty line. So families with children are more likely than single adults to be poor. Single-parent families, mostly headed by women, are especially likely to fall into poverty.

GLOBAL INEQUALITY

Wealth and income differ greatly among Americans, but the gap between rich and poor is tiny compared to the level of inequality among all the people of the world. According to Oxfam International (a charitable organization focused on global poverty), the eight richest people on Earth have as much wealth as the poorest 3.6 billion people—half the world's population. Together, the world's 1,810 billionaires have a net worth equal to the wealth of 70 percent of humanity.

Poverty is widespread in the United States, but it is far worse in most other nations. The World Bank (which lends money to groups that build housing, irrigation systems, schools, and other facilities in poor nations) sets the global poverty line at the equivalent

> The eight richest people on Earth have as much wealth as the poorest 3.6 billion people—half the world's population.

of $1.90 (US dollars) per person each day. That adds up to just $693.50 a person a year. Anyone in any country who is living on this amount or less is said to be in absolute poverty. How does someone survive on $1.90 a day? It couldn't be done in the United States. Food and housing are far too expensive. But in some poor nations, such as those of central and southern Africa, it is possible to survive on this income—just barely. Millions of people in nations in Africa, South America, and Asia live on the streets or in makeshift shelters. They are hungry or malnourished. According to World Bank statistics, almost half the people on Earth—more than three billion people—live on less than $2.50 a day.

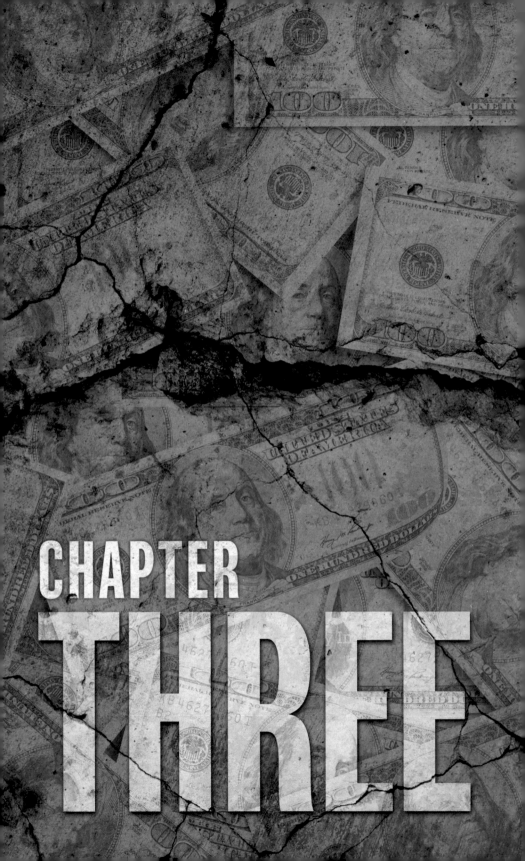

CHAPTER

THREE

THE COSTS OF INEQUALITY

Economists say that economic inequality isn't all bad. Societies with certain individuals earning more than others are marked by entrepreneurship. The desire to get rich can motivate workers to put in their best effort, think creatively, take risks, develop their skills, and sacrifice current comfort for future gains. If people in a society get the same financial reward no matter what they do, then why bother to work hard or innovate?

When workers have good jobs, they have more money to spend. They buy cars and other consumer goods. This spending brings more money to businesses, which can then hire more employees and raise wages.

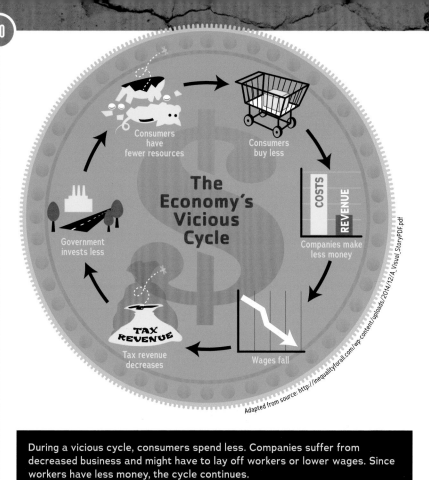

The Economy's Vicious Cycle

Consumers have fewer resources

Consumers buy less

Companies make less money

Wages fall

Tax revenue decreases

Government invests less

TAX REVENUE

Adapted from source: http://inequalityforall.com/wp-content/uploads/2014/12/A_Visual_StoryPDF.pdf

During a vicious cycle, consumers spend less. Companies suffer from decreased business and might have to lay off workers or lower wages. Since workers have less money, the cycle continues.

However, most economists say that in any nation, economic inequality shouldn't be too great or the overall economy will suffer. When the gap between rich and poor is large, only a small number of people have great wealth and the vast majority of people have very little wealth. Those with little wealth—rank-and-file consumers—have less money to spend.

When consumers spend less, businesses suffer. They might have to lay off workers or cut their pay. Since less money is changing hands in this scenario, less money goes to the government as taxes. The government can't provide as many services to citizens, and everyone is worse off. People tighten their belts and spend even less money, which translates into more losses for businesses, more layoffs, and more poverty. This is what economists call a vicious cycle.

The opposite—a virtuous cycle—results when economic inequality is low. When good-paying jobs are plentiful, more consumers have money to spend, which leads to business growth, more hiring, and more workers with money to spend.

CAPITALISM AND SOCIALISM ◄---------

The United States is primarily a capitalist economy. In a capitalist economic system, privately owned businesses provide most of the goods and services, and they operate to make a profit. Companies compete with one another for customers. Those companies that do a good job of providing things consumers want, at prices consumers are willing to pay, make money. Companies that don't make money usually go out of business.

In a capitalist system, government does not usually tell businesses what goods or services to make, how much to sell them for, or how much (above the minimum wage) to pay workers. Government does impose some regulations on business operations. For instance, in the United States, businesses that provide food and medicines must follow government rules about food and drug safety.

In a Socialist economic system, by contrast, the government owns many of the largest companies. They make goods and provide services to citizens. The government decides what products to make, how much goods and services will cost, and how much workers get paid.

No country is purely Socialist or purely capitalist. The US economy is based on capitalism. The United States also has some Socialist, government-run programs for the good of society. They include Medicare (health care for the elderly and some younger people with serious health issues or disabilities), Social Security (retirement, disability, and survivors' benefits), and welfare programs that provide food, housing, and other assistance to the poor.

THE VIRTUOUS CYCLE

The economy encompasses all the production, distribution, and consumption of goods and services in a country, or all that is made, sold, and bought. The monetary value of all the goods and services produced in a country within a certain period, such as one year, is called the gross domestic product (GDP).

Consumer spending accounts for about 70 percent of economic activity in the United States. When consumers spend money—when they pay their bills, go shopping, eat at restaurants, go on vacation, get their hair cut, pay for a class at the gym, have their devices repaired, download music and apps, go to the movies, buy gas, and hire

WHO ARE THE JOB CREATORS? ←-------

Not everyone agrees that middle-class spending creates jobs. Some politicians and business leaders say that members of the 1 percent are the job creators. They point out that no one can start a business or hire anyone without money. They say that banks and wealthy investors lend money to people with new business ideas and to companies that want to expand and hire more employees. Therefore, the best way to grow the economy and create new jobs, according to some, is to cut taxes on the wealthy. This gives them more money to invest and results in more businesses and more jobs.

The wealthy do invest in businesses, and this investment does create jobs. However, the wealthy tend to invest a relatively small percentage of their money in projects that hire American workers. A much larger portion of their investments goes to overseas projects.

Critics of the "job creators" concept say cutting taxes on the rich is not the most effective way of promoting job growth. They argue that cutting taxes on the poor and middle class (who will spend nearly all their extra money) or hiring workers for government projects—such as building new roads, bridges, and other infrastructure—creates more jobs per dollar spent.

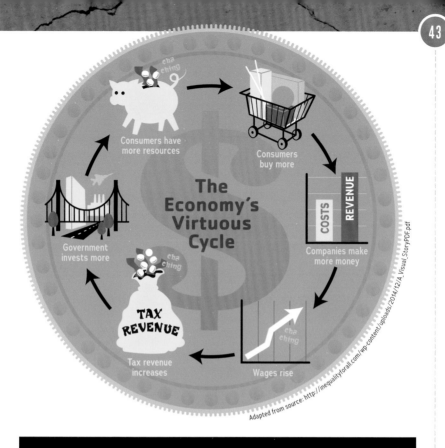

The Economy's Virtuous Cycle

Consumers have more resources

Consumers buy more

COSTS REVENUE
Companies make more money

Wages rise

TAX REVENUE
Tax revenue increases

Government invests more

Adapted from source: http://inequalityforall.com/wp-content/uploads/2014/12/A_Visual_StoryPDF.pdf

A virtuous cycle begins when workers have good wages. They spend most of that money, and that spending helps businesses.

babysitters—the economy grows. Businesses make money. They hire more workers to produce more goods and provide more services. They usually give raises to the employees they already have so that they don't leave for better jobs elsewhere.

Federal, state, and local governments also benefit from buying and selling. Governments collect taxes from many types of economic transactions, including the sale of goods, the incomes workers earn, and the profits companies make. Therefore, as the economy grows, tax revenues go up. This money allows the government to provide more services for citizens, such as building new roads and bridges, and to hire more employees to provide these services.

Spending creates jobs, and more jobs means more people have money to spend. And more money to spend means more buying, and more buying means more production and more jobs, and on and on. This is the virtuous cycle, but it can only operate when many citizens have good wages. When only a small number of workers earn a lot of money and the majority of workers have low pay, a vicious cycle can set in.

BIG SPENDERS

Since spending is good for the US economy, it's logical to ask: Why does it matter if some people have a lot more money than others? Don't rich people spend a lot of money? Enough to keep the economy rolling? The answer is yes, rich people spend a lot of money. They buy a lot of luxury items—such as sports cars and palatial homes—that most people could never afford. They hire personal chefs, security guards, drivers, and live-in nannies. Some of them spend millions on clothes and jewelry. But the rich spend a much smaller proportion of their money than most people do. For example, in 2007 Bank of America CEO Kenneth Lewis earned nearly $100 million. To spend it all, he would have had to spend more than $270,000 per day. That translates to about $23,000 every hour, twelve hours a day, 365 days a year. That's hard to do!

Because they have so much money, the top 1 percent of earners save a lot of money—as much as one-quarter of what they make each year. In contrast, the lower 99 percent spend nearly everything. They need almost every penny to pay for food, housing, health care, and all their other expenses. All that consumer spending helps the economy.

So what if instead of paying Lewis $100 million a year, Bank of America hired two thousand additional employees? Let's say those two thousand people earned $50,000 each. Each of those employees would likely have spent almost all of that money over the course of the year.

> The lower 99 percent spend nearly everything. They need almost every penny to pay for food, housing, health care, and all their other expenses. All that consumer spending helps the economy.

Combined, they would have put much more money into the economy than Lewis did. In this way, a greater number of people earning and spending wages contributes more to an economy than does the spending of just a few superrich citizens.

THE HOUSING BUBBLE

Economists know that the economy slows when people don't have enough money to spend. One way to try to get the economy going again is to make it cheaper and easier for people to borrow money. When credit is easy and affordable to get from banks, more individuals and businesses take out loans. The loans are good for economic growth because they enable families to buy new homes, new cars, and other goods and services. Loans also allow entrepreneurs to start new businesses and allow companies to open new stores, build new factories, and employ more people.

The Federal Reserve (nicknamed the Fed) is the central bank of the United States. It determines the amount of interest that lenders can charge borrowers. By lowering the interest rate, the Fed makes it easier and cheaper for businesses and individuals to borrow money. This encourages borrowing and leads to more spending, which boosts the economy.

However, the availability of too much credit can create problems. Easy, affordable credit encourages some people to take on debt that they cannot actually afford and will not be able to pay back. For example, in the first decade of the twenty-first century, when interest rates were very low, the bottom 80 percent of Americans were spending, on average, 110 percent of their incomes. Some of this spending involved charging purchases on credit cards. But much of it involved real estate loans. Many people took out loans to buy new houses. Many more took out home equity loans. With this type of loan, a homeowner borrows money and uses the home as collateral, a guarantee that the money will be repaid. If the homeowner does not keep up with monthly loan payments, the lender can take the home itself as repayment.

Rich investors also took advantage of the easy credit. Many of them bought houses as investments rather than as residences. They bought the houses intending to sell them at a future date for a higher price to make a profit. Real estate prices had been rising steadily for years, so many bankers, experts, and buyers thought that buying and selling houses was an extremely safe and reliable way to make money. In fact, financial experts at the time believed that housing prices would never fall. However, they were soon proven wrong.

With so many people wanting to buy houses, sellers could ask for higher and higher prices and just about always find someone willing to buy. People who were thinking about buying a house in the next few years saw how quickly prices were rising and decided to try to buy immediately, before prices went up even more. Meanwhile, investors also saw how quickly prices were rising and decided to buy more houses so they could sell them and cash in on the trend.

Demand for houses grew and grew. Builders put up new houses at a fast clip. Because it takes more than six months to construct a house, builders couldn't keep up with demand. With more people wanting to buy than houses available, housing prices rose even more. In one extreme example, home prices in Tampa, Florida, rose by 180 percent between 2000 and 2006. That is, housing prices nearly doubled in only six years.

Workers' salaries did not double at the same time, however, so many ordinary families who wanted to buy a home could not afford one. However, for real estate investors who were buying and selling houses, and for banks that were making huge amounts of money charging interest on home loans, business was booming. To continue making even more money, banks encouraged people to take out loans that they could not actually afford. Often banks were so eager to sign up borrowers that they didn't even ask for proof of income or verify that buyers would be able to pay back the loan.

And many banks didn't care if some buyers didn't pay back their loans because these banks were selling huge groups of the mortgages to investors (including other banks). Even if a few of the loans in the group were faulty, the investors would still make money from the interest payments from all the other loans in the bundle. Some of the loans in the bundles were insured, so if the borrower couldn't pay the money back, the insurance company would pay instead. Banks and investment firms made huge profits on these transactions—for a while.

THE BUBBLE BURSTS

In 2006 the bubble burst. Millions of homeowners were unable to keep up with their mortgage payments. Over the next few years, investors lost huge amounts of money when their mortgage bundles became worthless. Insurance companies could not afford to cover all the losses.

> In 2006 the bubble burst. Millions of homeowners were unable to keep up with their mortgage payments.

The owners of this home in Miami, Florida, couldn't pay their mortgage. The bank foreclosed on the mortgage, took possession of the home, and put it up for sale in 2009. The owners were one of millions who lost their homes during the housing crash.

When a borrower stops making payments on a loan, the bank can take possession of the house and foreclose. The homeowner must vacate the house and can lose all or some of the money invested in the home, depending on the circumstances. A California electrician named Dan was a victim of foreclosure. When Dan and his wife decided to buy a house, they determined that, based on their income, they could afford to pay $2,700 each month for their mortgage. They took out a bank loan. They believed their monthly mortgage payments would be $2,700. But after two months, the bill suddenly jumped from $2,700 to $3,600. Dan and his wife contacted the mortgage broker, the man who had arranged the loan with the bank. He told them that their initial payments were based on a "teaser rate" and that their actual interest rate was much higher. The broker hadn't made this clear when Dan and his wife agreed to the loan. When they could not keep up with the higher payments, the bank took their home.

Banks lend money and provide other financial services. But they are not in the business of owning houses or renting them to tenants. When banks foreclose on homes, they sometimes immediately put them up for sale—often at bargain prices. By selling foreclosed homes cheaply and quickly, banks can recoup at least some of the money they lent to these homeowners. Banks are insured, and sometimes, their insurance policies make up the difference, paying the banks the money they lose on foreclosed houses.

Housing prices peaked in 2006. Shortly thereafter, many banks began to sell foreclosed homes. Meanwhile, many homeowners who were struggling with their mortgage payments decided to sell their houses before they went into foreclosure. Suddenly far more houses were for sale than there were people to buy them. Prices began to fall and fast.

Bankers saw that their earlier shortsighted policies (lending too easily) and deceptive practices (holding back important information about loan terms) had backfired. They became much more cautious about offering loans, being more careful to verify income and looking more carefully at borrowers' financial situations. Under these conditions, even fewer people were able to qualify to borrow money to buy houses. Yet the supply of houses kept growing, even though the demand was decreasing. This drove down housing prices even more. The housing prices that had nearly doubled in Tampa took a nosedive, ending up even lower than they had been before the bubble.

More than nine million Americans lost their homes to foreclosure when the housing bubble burst. Many others ended up underwater— their houses were worth less than the amount they still owed on the mortgage. The damage was widespread. Even people who had already paid off their mortgages were affected. When housing prices dropped, so did the value of most homes. Suddenly poorer—either without a home, unable to keep up with mortgage payments, or with a much less valuable home—many people cut back on their spending. From

2007 to 2009, retail spending dropped by 8 percent, the second-largest decline in US history. This led to a downward economic spiral known as the Great Recession. Businesses lost money and cut back on hiring, and unemployment rose.

Big banks, real estate investors, and insurance companies lost so much money in the housing crash that by September 2008, some of them were on the verge of collapse. If the banks failed, every person or business with money in those banks would suddenly lose access to the cash. On the morning of September 18, 2008, US treasury secretary Hank Paulson said that if the US government didn't act immediately, $5.5 trillion in wealth would vanish by two o'clock that afternoon. Millions of people would be suddenly broke. Companies would no longer be able to pay their employees. The crisis, Paulson asserted, would set off a chain reaction that would crash the entire worldwide economy and lead to another Great Depression.

Big banks, real estate investors, and insurance companies lost so much money in the housing crash that by September 2008, some of them were on the verge of collapse.

To prevent complete disaster, the federal government stepped in. Under a project called the Troubled Asset Relief Program (TARP), Congress agreed to buy $700 billion in troubled mortgages (those for which payments were overdue). The plan was to renegotiate the terms of those loans, allowing homeowners to make smaller payments over longer periods with lower interest rates. This plan would help banks while also allowing millions of homeowners to keep their houses.

US treasury secretary Hank Paulson speaks about the financial crisis caused by the housing bubble in late 2008. Other government finance leaders look on including Ben Bernanke (*back, far left*), chairperson of the US Federal Reserve.

But that's not what happened. Misleading Congress, the Fed and the US Treasury altered the program into one that was more agreeable to Wall Street. Instead of buying bad mortgages and helping homeowners, the government lent the money directly to banks at low interest rates.

The plan continued to diverge from what Congress had approved. By 2012 the US government had spent more than $7.7 trillion bailing out banks, insurance companies, and other large corporations affected by the real estate crash. The companies had to pay back the loans, but they also benefited from reduced taxes and other provisions of the bailout. In the end, only about 1 percent of the money the government spent to save the economy went to help ordinary people keep their homes. The impact of the financial crisis fell most heavily on the 99 percent, and inequality rose even further.

Without a home of their own, a mom and her three kids stay at a temporary shelter in New York City. When the economy takes a downturn, unemployment rises. With no income to pay rent, some unemployed people become homeless.

THE HUMAN COSTS

Economic stagnation (lack of growth) and instability (bubbles and crashes) are large-scale economic problems. They have profound effects on the lives of real people.

Unemployment is the most immediate issue, since people without jobs usually cannot support themselves or their families. But high unemployment causes other problems as well. Employers might try to save money (and increase profits) by paying workers less, knowing that employees with few job options will be unlikely to quit and look for work elsewhere. Employers also might try to reduce workers' benefits, such as contributions to health insurance or retirement plans. To make ends meet under these circumstances, people may have to work multiple jobs. Many use credit cards or loans to pay bills. They go deeply into debt. They cannot save any money for retirement or to cover their bills during unemployment, a medical emergency, or another crisis.

Economic strain can have a lasting effect on family health. Health-care costs in the United States are higher than anywhere else in the world, and many Americans cannot afford health insurance or the care they need. They avoid going to the doctor and sometimes miss discovering serious health issues.

MARY LEE'S FALL ◄-----------------------------

Mary Lee, a resident of Washington State, is forty-eight years old and college educated. She was laid off when her company moved her job overseas. She started her own business, but it did not succeed. She ran out of money and could no longer afford rent or house payments. She survives by sleeping in her car or on friends' couches and eating cheap packages of ramen noodles. She describes her life this way:

I pretend it is not that bad to others. I wouldn't even tell my doctor at the low-income clinic how bad things are for me. I am too embarrassed to let anyone know that I sleep in my car and have only one pair of pants left to wear. I used to have a good income. I used to go hiking and work full time and walk my dog and jog five days a week. I had what many people have in America, and I took it for granted that I would always have a home and a job and enough money to at least pay the bills and keep my clothes clean and eat healthy food. I never touched Top Ramen [brand noodles] back in my 20s.

Yes, I do know that there are . . . many people worse off . . . than me, but until you experience this long-term poverty situation, you can't really understand how it devastates your ability to function and robs you of your health from the stress, the instability, and the lack of ability to eat healthy. I do my best, and still I am grateful for the basic things in life, even the Ramen noodles. . . . I don't see a way out of this situation at this time.

WHO'S IN THE LABOR FORCE? ◄-----------

Every month the federal government surveys Americans aged sixteen and older to determine the unemployment rate. The government considers the unemployed to be those people who do not currently have a job and have actively looked for work within the most recent four weeks. "Actively looking for work" means contacting an employer directly, going to a job interview, submitting resumes, filling out job applications, or visiting an employment agency. Reading job ads or attending a job training program does not count as actively looking for work. The survey labels those who are neither employed nor actively looking for work as "not in the labor force."

When the economy remains weak for an extended period, a number of people give up on finding a job and stop actively looking for work. They "fall out of the labor force," and they are no longer included in the unemployment rate. Most of those who have fallen out of the labor force depend upon family members to support them. Some turn to illegal activities such as dealing drugs. Some become homeless (*below*). After the economy recovers, workers who have fallen out of the labor force often have a hard time getting back in. When hiring, many employers prefer job candidates with a steady work history. They might be hesitant to hire someone who has not worked for many months or years. In this way, an economic downturn can cause harm and increase economic inequality for many years—even when the economy has recovered.

Fresh healthy food is expensive, so many poor Americans eat cheaper, prepackaged, high-fat, high-salt foods with less nutritional value. Stress, such as constantly worrying about money, can lead to high blood pressure, anxiety, and depression. Men in the top 1 percent have fewer worries about money and live, on average, more than fourteen years longer than financially strained men in the bottom 1 percent. For women, the difference is about ten years.

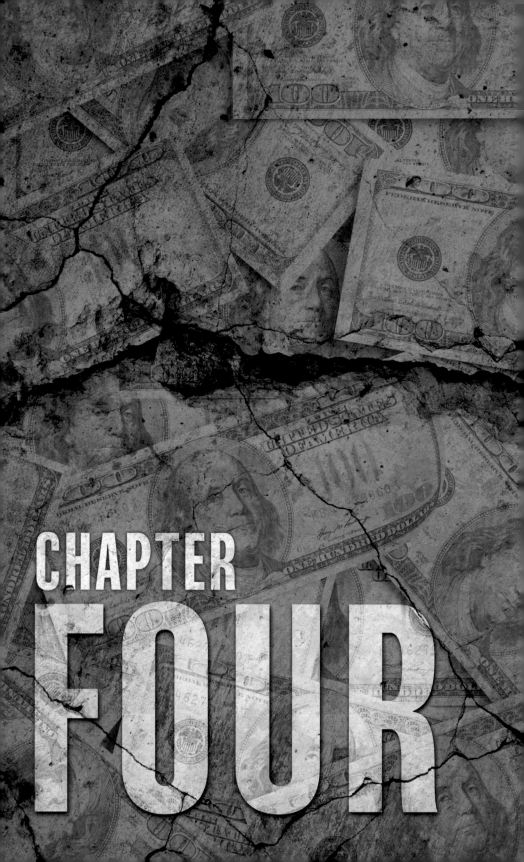

CHAPTER
FOUR

INEQUALITY OF OPPORTUNITY

Horatio Alger, a popular American writer of the late nineteenth century, is famous for his rags-to-riches stories. In books like *Ragged Dick*, Alger's young male heroes succeed through a combination of luck and pluck. In fact, *Luck and Pluck* is the title of one of his books. In each book, the main character starts out poor, but he is hardworking, honest, cheerful, and determined. His goodness brings him to the attention of a wealthy benefactor. This gentleman takes an interest in the boy, gives him a job or provides him with money to invest, introduces him to important people, and paves the young man's path to success.

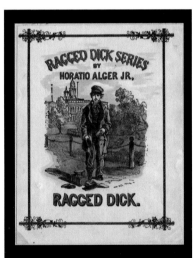

In his *Ragged Dick* series of books, Horatio Alger promoted the idea that anyone who works hard can succeed in the United States. The reality is that those born into poverty are less likely to succeed, no matter how hard they work.

These stories are fantasies. And fantasy is at the heart of the American Dream—the idea that any enterprising American can become rich and achieve his or her life's goals, regardless of social class. US historian James Truslow Adams coined the term in his 1932 book *The Epic of America*. In reality, the American Dream is not accessible to everyone. Whether you succeed in the United States depends a lot on where you grow up, how much money your parents have, what gender you are, and what color your skin is.

MEASURING THE AMERICAN DREAM

Social mobility is the movement of people (upward or downward) within or between different economic groups—the poor, the middle class, and the wealthy. Social scientists identify two types of social mobility—absolute mobility and relative mobility.

Absolute upward mobility occurs when adult children have more education, higher incomes, or both than their parents do. To assess absolute upward mobility, economists evaluate people's incomes and education levels around aged thirty or forty, once they have had a chance to complete school and establish a career. Economists then adjust the income numbers for inflation. This adjustment allows economists to accurately compare a parent's income at the age of thirty to a child's income at the same age, two or three decades later.

Tracking absolute mobility is one way to see how a society as a whole is doing. Is the population generally getting richer and better educated, staying about the same, or getting poorer? If the economy is growing and access to education is expanding, absolute upward mobility can theoretically occur for everyone in society at the same time.

Absolute upward mobility in the United States was high during the period of strong economic growth and educational expansion following World War II. Children born in 1940 (near the end of the Great Depression) had a 92 percent chance of earning more than their parents. However, absolute upward mobility has been on the decline since then. Only half of the children born in 1980 earned more at the age of thirty than their parents earned at that age. American parents once took it for granted that their children would have more income and wealth than they did. But in the twenty-first century, many Americans struggle just to maintain a similar standard of living to what they had growing up.

Social scientists also track and analyze relative mobility. Relative mobility has to do with whether families remain wealthy or remain poor from generation to generation. If it didn't matter who your parents were and every child had an equal chance of success—regardless of class, gender, race, or ethnicity—then plenty of poor children would grow up to be rich and plenty of rich children would grow up to be poor. When lots of people end up in a different social class (either upward or downward) than the one they were born into, social scientists say a society has high relative mobility.

ISAAC'S MIRACLE ◄---------------------------

Isaac's mother died when he was five, and he never knew his father. His grandparents raised him in Denver, Colorado, in a neighborhood that was once home to the largest iron factory in North America. That and other industries had polluted the soil and air. Like most of the kids at his school, Isaac came from a low-income family, so he qualified for free school lunch, paid for by the federal government.

Despite his economic disadvantages, Isaac graduated from college and went on to study education policy at the prestigious Teachers College at Columbia University in New York City. "Sometimes I think it's a miracle how far I have come," he says. "A little, skinny Latino kid who grew up in one of Denver's poorest and most polluted neighborhoods is now a graduate student at [a prestigious] university." He credits his success to mentoring and support from key adults in his life. "I had a strong and unwavering support system that included great mentors, excellent traditional public school teachers and counselors, and two wonderful grandparents. I had a group of people who never gave up on helping me succeed, no matter how daunting the odds looked."

Despite the idea that the United States is the land of opportunity, studies have consistently found that the United States is one of the least economically mobile of the world's industrialized nations. Studies reveal that if you grow up poor in the United States, you are likely to be poor as an adult. If you grow up middle class, you are likely to stay middle class, and if you grow up rich, you will likely remain rich. The exceptions are rare. Why?

YOU ARE WHERE YOU LIVE

US neighborhoods tend to be segregated by income as well as by race. For example, many rich white families live in mansions in exclusive gated communities. Many upper-middle-class families, mostly white, live in suburbs or on the outskirts of big cities, where lawns are big and schools are well funded. Well-to-do neighborhoods offer a lot of perks to their residents. They generally enjoy well-maintained parks, well-funded schools and libraries, clean streets, and thriving business districts.

But many poor Americans, including large numbers of Hispanics, American Indians, and African Americans, live in run-down, inner-city neighborhoods with no green spaces and poorly funded schools. Some rural regions of the United States are also very poor, although these areas tend to have small populations.

Living in poverty is never easy, and living in a poor neighborhood is especially difficult. Businesses are reluctant to set up shop in poor or declining neighborhoods. Families in these areas have few services and have to travel long distances to shop for household goods. Lack of local businesses also means that poor families don't have as many food options as wealthier areas. Many inner-city neighborhoods lack full-service grocery stores, where shoppers can find fresh fruits, vegetables, and other healthy foods. Inner-city families rely instead on convenience stores and fast-food outlets, which generally offer high-fat, high-sugar, and prepackaged foods. These types of foods lead to obesity and other

A man repairs his car in the South Bronx, an area of New York City. Poor, inner-city neighborhoods lack many stores and services. Residents often have to travel far to buy groceries and gas or visit a doctor.

health problems. Poor neighborhoods also have fewer doctor's offices and health clinics than wealthier areas.

Without nearby employers, residents have to commute to other parts of the city for work. If they own a car, they have to battle traffic and use their limited income to pay car maintenance, gas, and insurance. Those without cars must rely on public transportation to get to their jobs. However, many big US cities don't have enough buses, trains, and other forms of public transit to serve the community. Or they don't have enough money to keep the vehicles in good repair and running smoothly. Many inner-city dwellers face long commutes, delays, and inconvenient routes and drop-off points. Such transportation hassles can make it difficult for an employee to succeed on the job.

Many poor neighborhoods are near industrial areas, where factories, power plants, and other industries have polluted the air, water,

ELIJAH'S HORROR ←----------------------

Twenty-four-year-old Elijah grew up in a very poor part of New Orleans, Louisiana. He hated his neighborhood, where drug abuse, homelessness, and violence were all around him. "When I was four years old," he recalls, "I seen this pretty little girl, rolling on her little scooter, die in the drive-by [shooting]. Just out of nowhere. The next thing you know, I see her jump crazy with blood, shot through the forehead." Elijah told an interviewer, "Every time my grandfather would take me to see a scary movie, it wouldn't scare me at all, because I seen worse. Go outside, I'll show you what's scary."

and soil. Exposure to environmental pollution can lead to asthma (a chronic lung disease), cancer, and other severe illnesses. In some poor communities, city water supplies are contaminated with lead and other toxins. Because it is often unsafe for children in poor neighborhoods to play outside, whether because of violence or environmental hazards, they get less exercise than children with big yards and welcoming, safe parks nearby. All this adds up to poor health for poor children. The American Academy of Pediatrics says, "Poor children have increased infant mortality [death rates]; more frequent and severe chronic diseases such as asthma; poorer nutrition and growth; less access to quality health care . . . and increased obesity." Teenage pregnancy is also higher in poor neighborhoods because poor teenagers have less access to birth control than their wealthier peers. Poor teens may not have a regular doctor, for example, may not have health insurance, or may not be able to afford birth control.

EDUCATION—THE GREAT EQUALIZER?

The American public education system is the backbone of the claim that the nation provides equal opportunity for all. Every child in the nation, rich or poor, is guaranteed thirteen years of free education. Public schools are meant to prepare all American youth for the next stage in a productive life, such as going to college or starting a job. Yet the promise doesn't match reality. From day care through university, children of different economic backgrounds receive educations of vastly different quality. And some children get barely any education at all.

When children start kindergarten, certain skills will help them succeed in the classroom. These skills include the ability to carry on a conversation with an adult, sit still to listen to a story, and answer basic questions about the story afterward. Those kindergartners who know colors, the alphabet, and the sounds of at least some of the letters also have a good basis for success.

Children from educated, privileged families usually have all these skills when they start kindergarten. But children from underprivileged families generally start school without many of these skills. This is not because poor children are less smart. It's because they have had fewer chances to develop these skills, which require practice over time with an adult or older sibling.

Parents are similar in many ways. Regardless of how much money they make or how much education they have, most parents play with and talk to their kids. They try to provide them with toys, teach them good manners and conversation skills, build their confidence and self-respect, and help them learn to feed, dress, and take care of themselves. However, studies have found that richer, more educated parents talk to their children more than do poorer, less educated parents. Language develops through experience, so it matters that on average, children from poor families hear about half as many words an hour (roughly six hundred) as children from working-class families (twelve hundred words an hour) and less than one-third as many words as children from professional families (twenty-one hundred words an hour). For this reason, privileged children develop bigger vocabularies. At the age of three, children from professional families know about 1,116 different words, compared to 749 for working-class children and 525 for poor children. Having a strong vocabulary and good language skills is vital for school and workplace success, so this deficit puts poor children at a significant and lasting disadvantage.

Another major disadvantage for low-income children is that their lives tend to be extremely stressful. Trying to feed a family, pay the rent, and cover other bills without enough money puts enormous pressure on parents. Some of this stress affects their children, no matter how much parents try to shield them. Furthermore, studies have found that low-income children are more likely to live with trauma, such as parental mental illness, unstable families, abuse, and neglect. These and other difficult situations trigger the release of the body's stress hormones, including cortisol. When cortisol levels remain high for extended periods, they affect brain development, particularly in young children. As a result, children with traumatic home lives can find it difficult to concentrate, remember information, and sit still. Stress hormones also weaken the body's ability to fight off disease, making low-income children more likely to get sick and miss school.

High-quality day care and preschool programs provide kids with practice in preliteracy skills and a safe, stable, and calm environment for learning and growing. But these programs can be far too expensive for many families. Costs vary a lot from state to state and from program to program. In most places in the United States, families with two young children pay more for day care than they do for rent. Because of the high cost of child care, many women cannot afford to remain in the workforce after they have children. A mother working for the median minimum state wage ($7.75 an hour) would have to devote all her income from January to September to pay for one year of infant care.

Some US government programs, such as the federal Head Start program, offer preschool for low-income children and support services for their parents. But these programs do not have enough funding to accommodate all the children who qualify for enrollment. In the end,

Preschoolers play at a Head Start program in Fairfax, Virginia. Preschool helps prepare children for success in elementary school. But most preschool programs are too expensive for many working families.

children who don't get a leg up through preschool programs tend to be behind their peers when they enter elementary school. And catching up over the years can be nearly impossible.

POOR KIDS GO TO POOR SCHOOLS

Privileged children and underprivileged children enter school with very different skills. They also enter very different types of schools.

Public schools use a combination of federal, state, and local funds to pay teachers; buy books, computers, and other equipment; and keep buildings in good working order. Nearly half of the money comes from local property taxes. Each year property owners must pay a percentage of the value of their homes to one or more local governments (such as a county or city) as property taxes. Communities with lots of expensive houses (and usually mostly white residents) collect a lot of money in property taxes—money that they can pour into their schools. Communities filled with inexpensive, run-down properties collect

A MODEL FOR HOPE:
THE ABECEDARIAN PROJECT ◄------------

The Abecedarian Project, run by the University of North Carolina at Chapel Hill, has provided some of the best evidence for the long-term benefits of early childhood programs. In 1972 the project recruited 111 children from low-income families to participate in a study. Most of the children were African American.

About half of the children (fifty-seven) were randomly assigned to attend day care. The other fifty-four children were the control (comparative) group. They received no day care and were later compared to the children who did.

The children in the day care group received full-time care, five days a week, twelve months a year, from early infancy until they entered kindergarten at the age of five. They received regular medical care on-site. The teachers played with each child, using games designed to encourage social, emotional, mental, and physical development. Teachers especially emphasized language. "We told the teachers that every game is a language game," remembers Joseph Sparling, one of the designers and administrators of the program. "Even if the activity focused mostly on motor [physical] skills, the teachers still needed to talk to the children and to [encourage] age-appropriate language from them."

The results from this program have been long-lasting and significant. Compared to the control group, the children who participated in the Abecedarian Project had higher math and reading scores throughout elementary and secondary school. They were also less likely to be held back a grade or to be put in special education programs. They were more likely to have graduated from college by the age of thirty and less likely to have become parents at a very young age. They were also healthier, possibly because of their early medical care and because having support in early childhood lowered their stress levels.

much less money in property taxes. Poor neighborhoods therefore end up with poor schools. They have little money, so they can't pay for expensive technology, highly qualified teachers, and current books. This means the schools can't offer a good, up-to-date education.

Some states make the education system fairer by pooling taxes from rich and poor communities. That way, all schools across the state receive the same amount of money per pupil. Fifteen states go even further, redistributing property taxes—they give more money per student to high-poverty schools than to schools that serve well-off students. Supporters of this system say that privileged children tend to have much more support, guidance, and stimulation outside of school than do underprivileged children. They come to school with many advantages. So the extra money for high-poverty schools is one way to level the playing field for students there, to make up for some of the disadvantages they face.

However, in nearly half of all states, property taxes are not redistributed. Rich communities heap money on their pupils, while poor neighborhoods must get by with what they have. This means that rich students enjoy schools with plenty of new computers, up-to-date textbooks, well-stocked libraries, art and music classes, athletic fields and equipment, gifted and talented programs, small class sizes, and plenty of experienced teachers and guidance counselors. Poor students are more likely to go to school in older buildings with few working computers, out-of-date books, overcrowded classrooms, inadequate help for students with special needs, overworked and underpaid teachers, and counselors with huge caseloads.

One teacher in Connecticut who moved from a poor school to a rich school told the *Atlantic* magazine that misbehaving students in her old school were often suspended because teachers and guidance counselors were simply too overloaded to deal with them. The suspended students missed a lot of school and fell behind their classmates. In her new school, the teacher has time to work with children who get into trouble, helping them change their behavior while staying in school, rather than suspending them.

PAYING THE PRICE

The funding differences between schools can have a lifetime of repercussions for students. Consider those kids who were suspended because their teachers and counselors didn't have the resources to help them improve their behavior. Research shows that kids who miss school, whether because of suspension or truancy (being absent without an excuse), are more likely to fail individual classes. Those who fail classes are less likely to graduate from high school. In the twenty-first century, most jobs require at least a high school degree. Without one, young adults have few options other than dead-end, low-skill, low-paying jobs.

As an alternative to barely surviving on low-level wages, some people in poor neighborhoods turn to crime, which can lead to jail or prison time. Others live on the streets or abuse drugs. Most poor communities don't have enough job training programs, substance abuse treatment programs, and other social services to help these struggling residents get their lives back on track.

Race plays a big part in this dilemma. For example, even though the percentages of whites, Hispanics, and blacks who use illegal drugs are similar, blacks and Hispanics are much more likely than whites to be arrested and imprisoned for drug crimes. So the US prison population is disproportionately black and Hispanic. Those who face a bleak future in poor inner-city neighborhoods also tend to be people of color.

IT'S NOT JUST ABOUT THE MONEY

Students who attend well-funded schools—including private schools, charter schools, and public schools in rich neighborhoods—generally perform much better than students in poor schools. For example, sixth graders in the richest school districts in the United States are four grade levels ahead of sixth graders in the poorest districts in math and reading. Those differences aren't related only to differences in school funding. Parents who are well-off are often actively involved in their children's schools. They use their social and business connections to raise money for extracurricular activities, field trips, and special equipment. They might not have to work full-time so they volunteer in classrooms, helping with extracurricular events and activities. The parents' professional backgrounds give them skills, connections, and confidence to help their children. They also put more pressure on teachers and principals to provide a good education for their kids.

They also make sure their children come to school prepared to learn. Children with well-educated parents usually have strong reading and math skills. Their parents expect them to do well in school and to continue on to college. Students at affluent schools provide

Students collaborate during an engineering class at a high school in Marlborough, Massachusetts. Residents of wealthy communities pay high property taxes, and this money helps fund well-equipped, fully staffed schools.

one another with a good learning environment. They pressure one another to do well. The competition can be stressful, but it encourages students to push themselves and helps them succeed. In contrast, parents of children in poor schools may not have the same professional advantages. They don't have the time or professional connections to raise money for the school or the skills to volunteer in a classroom. They may work several part-time jobs and not have time to help their kids with homework.

For both students and teachers, the atmosphere in poor schools can be toxic. Violence and drug abuse may be common and hard to control. Children who have come to school unprepared with basic skills are more likely to become angry, frustrated, and hopeless. Many decide that they are stupid and lose confidence and self-esteem. Others decide that school is not worth the effort, particularly when they look around them and see little hope of going to college or getting a good job. In neighborhoods and schools where poverty is everywhere, residents can find it extremely difficult to find support and opportunities to break out and build a better life.

HIGHER EDUCATION: HARD TO PAY FOR

In the twenty-first century, good-paying jobs generally require a college education. And a college degree makes a huge difference in earnings. In 2014 median weekly pay for those with a high school degree was $668, while those with a bachelor's degree or higher earned a median weekly wage of $1,193. Those without a high school degree are more likely to have no job at all.

Graduating from college is key to good earnings, but for poor and even middle-income young people, a college education is often out of reach. In part, this is because the public education system does a poor job of preparing low-income students for college. Another problem is cost. A year of tuition and fees at a public, in-state, four-year university averaged more than $9,600 in 2016–2017. Out-of-state and private universities are roughly three times more expensive. And regardless of the type of institution, room and board add $10,000 or more a year. Books, computers, and other expenses up the cost even more.

Some students and their families receive financial help to pay for college. Federal and state governments, colleges and universities, and private institutions offer financial aid. This can be grants (government funds that do not have to be paid back), tax breaks, work-study jobs, scholarships, and student loans. However, tuition has been steadily increasing since the 1980s, while grants and scholarships have not kept up. To make up the difference, the amount of borrowing to pay for college has ballooned. Upon graduation from a four-year institution, the average student borrower in the class of 2015 owed slightly more than $35,000. This is more than twice what graduates in 1995 owed, adjusted for inflation.

College students with loans do not necessarily realize how burdensome the debt can be. School loans can take a decade or more to

As part of a protest in 2012, demonstrators wore signs showing the amount of student debt they owed. Many students borrow vast sums of money to pay for college.

pay off. During that time, borrowers have less money for housing, food, transportation, entertainment, and savings. Student loan debt may also influence career choices. Borrowers may feel pressured to choose a better-paying or more secure job than one that is personally fulfilling or socially useful.

Even when a person has a steady job, making the monthly loan payments can be difficult. In 2015 nearly one-third of borrowers in the United States were at least one month behind on their student loan payments. Missing a payment or having a large amount of debt

VERONICA'S DEBT ←--------------------

Veronica is the first person in her family to go to college. She attends a small, public university in Kansas. She deliberately chose one of the most affordable four-year schools in her state. Even so, she had to borrow $33,000 to pay for everything she needed to make it through her junior year. She says,

> While I know students everywhere are bearing the weight of student loan debt, I was unprepared for the reality that clicking the accept button on the financial aid page was addicting and often necessary. I find this terrifying since I live in a city with a relatively low cost of living. Loans were not only how I paid for my tuition, but how I caught up my rent, how I made those annoying car repairs to keep it running, and how I bought food, soap, and the one new outfit I allowed myself each semester. I have so many regrets. My journalism major holds a bleak future [because paid journalism jobs are rare and becoming rarer] making me wish I would have taken more credit hours freshman year when I had scholarship money or not gone on the spring break trip that caused me to miss work. It's too late now; I feel like I am barely treading water to reach the 124 hours required to graduate. . . . I'm hoping one day I'll see what college has given me besides a $33,000 bill.

lowers a person's credit score. Credit scores are numerical ratings that represent how likely a person is to pay bills on time. Lenders use credit scores to determine whether to give someone a credit card, cell phone plan, car loan, mortgage, or other type of loan. Someone with a low credit score might be denied credit altogether or might have to pay a higher interest rate and higher fees than someone with a high credit score. In addition, applications for loans for a car, a house, and other trappings of comfortable middle-class life will probably be denied.

CHAPTER
FIVE

MONEY IS POWER

The US Declaration of Independence states firmly that the purpose of government is to protect the rights of the governed. The US government is meant to be, as President Abraham Lincoln put it in his famous 1863 Gettysburg Address, "of the people, for the people, and by the people." It is supposed to represent all Americans, regardless of who they are—and certainly regardless of how much money a person has.

President Abraham Lincoln stressed in 1863 that the United States has a government "for the people and by the people." However, in the twenty-first century, rich people are much more likely to vote and participate in government than are poor people.

WHAT DOES THE FEDERAL GOVERNMENT DO FOR US? ◄ ─ ─ ─ ─ ─ ─ ─ ─ ─ ─ ─ ─ ─ ─ ─ ─ ─ ─ ─

Governments at all levels (city, county, state, and federal) use tax money to provide citizens with important services. In 2015 the federal government spent $3.7 trillion on such services. The government spent the largest portion of its budget ($938 billion, or about one-quarter of the budget) on health-care programs. These programs included Medicare, Medicaid, and subsidized individual insurance under the Affordable Care Act.

Nearly one-quarter of the federal budget ($888 billion) went to Social Security. About 16 percent of the federal budget ($602 billion) went to the US military to pay for weapons; the operation of military bases; ships, airplanes, and other vehicles; and salaries for military personnel. Programs to help the poor, such as food assistance and public housing, cost $362 billion. This was 10 percent of the budget.

Each year the federal government spends more money to pay for these programs than it receives in taxes, so it must borrow money to make up the difference. And like any other borrower, it must pay interest on that debt. In 2015 interest paid on the national debt was about $223 billion (6 percent of the federal budget).

The remaining 19 percent of the budget was split among benefits for veterans and retired federal workers (8 percent); transportation infrastructure, such as roads, bridges, and airports (2 percent); education (3 percent); science and medical research (2 percent); humanitarian aid, such as food and medicine for people in poor nations (1 percent); and all other programs (3 percent).

The United States spends about $602 billion per year on military operations. This includes paying soldiers and training military working dogs.

Reality falls far short of this ideal, however. The very wealthy in the United States have an outsized influence over what the government does. When the public is divided about what direction government should take, lawmakers must pick a side. According to research by Martin Gilens, professor of politics at Princeton University in New Jersey, when the richest 10 percent and the poorest 10 percent strongly disagree about an issue, the rich always win. The same is true for the middle class. When they strongly disagree with the top 10 percent, the government listens to the rich, not the middle class.

We all have a guaranteed right to inform the government of our wants, needs, and opinions. When we elect representatives, each person gets a single vote. So why do the interests of the wealthy few outweigh the needs of the poorer many?

THE WELL-OFF ARE MORE POLITICALLY ACTIVE

In theory, every adult citizen in the United States has an equal right to vote. However, not everyone who is eligible to vote ends up voting. Poverty and racism are at the root of this reality. Studies show that the more money an American has, the more likely that person is to vote. At the top of the income scale, the voting rate is 80 percent. Of the poorest Americans, fewer than 50 percent vote. Because of this voting behavior, the pool of voters is weighted toward the wealthy. In 2014 only about one in five Americans made more than $100,000 a year, but nearly one-third of active voters earned that much.

Why are the poor less likely to vote? Poor people understand that the government is unlikely to be swayed by their opinions. They see that elected officials pay more attention to the interests of the wealthy than the interests of the poor. This knowledge alone discourages many poor people from voting. Some laws also make it harder for people of color, young Americans, and poor people to cast votes. In the past, some states imposed poll taxes, which required voters to pay to cast their ballots. Poll taxes were especially common in states with large African American communities. Because African Americans were mostly poor, they could not afford the fee and couldn't vote. In some states, election officials handed out a series of test questions to voters. The tests weren't required of everyone—election officials could administer them at their own discretion, and they usually required only black Americans to take the tests. The tests asked difficult questions about US law and government. Those who didn't pass weren't allowed to vote, and many poorly educated black Americans failed the tests. In this way, the tests further disenfranchised (deprived of voting rights) African Americans.

The civil rights movement of the twentieth century fought to right these injustices. For example, the Twenty-Fourth Amendment to the US Constitution, ratified in 1964, abolished poll taxes, and the Civil Rights Act of 1964 prohibited knowledge tests for voters. But in the twenty-first century, some states have enacted new laws that make it difficult for poor Americans to vote. These voter identification (ID) laws require people to provide a photo ID, such as a driver's license, before they can vote. In many states, voters are also required to prove that they are legal citizens of the United States. Critics argue that these laws discriminate against the poor, immigrants, and people of color. For example, many inner-city residents do not have driver's licenses because they cannot afford cars. Some states offer and accept other types of government-issued identification, but these can be difficult to obtain. Offices that issue such ID might have limited hours. They may be in faraway suburbs that are difficult or time-consuming to reach by public transportation. Estimates for the number of eligible voters in the United States without a form of government-issued ID range from 1 percent to 11 percent. Voter ID laws reduce turnout mostly among black and Hispanic voters. They are more likely to be poor, to lack access to a car, and to face the most obstacles to obtaining an ID.

States also suppress voting by restricting the voting rights of felons.

In twenty-four states, convicted felons are not allowed to vote for some years after release from prison. In an additional ten states, some felons permanently lose their voting rights. In the 2014 congressional election, for example, 3.5 million Americans were barred from voting due to these policies. Critics of the policies say that those who have finished their prison sentences should not be further penalized with the loss of their constitutional right to vote. Critics also note that the rules most heavily penalize people of color. The US prison population is disproportionately black and Hispanic, so an outsized portion of those disenfranchised because of a felony conviction are people of color.

THINNING THE VOTER LIST

Purging voter rolls also tends to disenfranchise certain people. Purging the rolls involves removing names from a list of eligible voters if those people have died or if their address no longer matches the address on the registration list. This is cumbersome, time-consuming, and expensive and often introduces error. Sometimes names of people who are eligible to vote are removed, and when they arrive at the polls, they are blocked from voting. Such policies tend to disenfranchise young adults (who move often), as well as poor people who can't afford their own house or apartment. Purging the rolls also disproportionately affects women, since women often change their last names when they get married or divorced.

Some voters, especially poor, elderly, and disabled Americans, have difficulty making it to the polls on Election Day. They might not have a way to get there. Or they might be physically frail or only able to reach the polls in a vehicle that can accommodate a wheelchair. In some states, employers are not required to give workers time off to vote, so workers there might skip voting because they can't make time for it and still show up for work. To make it easier, thirty-five states allow early voting, a period several weeks ahead of Election Day when voters can cast ballots at their convenience at designated polling places. But in

At the 2008 presidential election, voters in Birmingham, Alabama, stood in long lines to cast their ballots. When lines are very long, some voters get discouraged and decide not to vote.

states without early voting, many people—unable to get to the polls on Election Day—do not vote.

Other obstacles include densely populated neighborhoods, where voters have to stand in long lines at polling places. In the 2016 presidential election, for example, some voters had to wait two hours or more to vote in Charlotte, North Carolina; Las Vegas, Nevada; and New York City. Many voters can't endure such a long wait. They must return to work or get home to care for their kids, so they leave. This issue impacts more than just a single election. Studies show that people who have to wait in long lines are less likely to vote in future elections.

A practice called gerrymandering has effectively disenfranchised many people of color in the United States. Gerrymandering involves dividing a city, state, or county into voting districts that favor one party over another. The word *gerrymandering* emerged in 1812 when the Massachusetts Legislature, under Governor Elbridge Gerry, created a voting district by grouping together counties where most people favored the Federalist political party. The Federalists were sure to win elections in that district, since it had been specifically created to contain a Federalist majority. Some observers thought that on a map, the strangely shaped district looked like a salamander. Others called it a gerrymander after the governor. Gerrymandering continues in the twenty-first century. For instance, in Wisconsin in 2010, Republican state lawmakers created voting districts that grouped together large blocks of Republican voters. Even though Democrats also lived in those districts, they were the minority and were sure to be outnumbered in elections for state legislators. In this case, the Democrats included large numbers of people of color. In 2015 a group of Wisconsin voters sued the state, charging that the gerrymandering there was racially biased and unconstitutional. In early October 2017, the US Supreme Court heard oral arguments in the case, *Gill v. Whitford*.

Bill Whitford is a retired University of Wisconsin law professor. He was the lead plaintiff in a 2017 US Supreme Court case that claimed that gerrymandering in the state of Wisconsin is extreme and deprives voters of a key principle of democratic government: one person, one vote.

Voter suppression is unconstitutional only if it can be proven that its purpose is to discriminate against certain racial groups. In some cases, courts have struck down discriminatory voter ID laws, voter purges, and other voter restriction measures. However, when states enact policies that disenfranchise certain groups, supporters usually claim that the measures are not designed to suppress the vote. They argue that the measures are intended to cut down on voter fraud, such as illegal voting by noncitizen immigrants. However, studies repeatedly show that voter fraud in the United States is almost nonexistent.

BIG SPENDERS

Voting is not the only way to participate in a democratic government. People can contact their elected representatives by writing, e-mailing, texting, or calling their offices. Citizens can also donate money to or volunteer to work for a political campaign or party. And citizens can express their views in marches, protests, and other public forums. Studies show that rich people are more likely to take part in such activities than are poor people. Americans in the top 20 percent of wealth devote 2.6 times as many hours to political activity as people in the bottom 20 percent. And wealthy Americans contribute 76 times as many dollars to political campaigns. The numbers make sense in that wealthy Americans have more money and can therefore contribute more to politicians. They are also more likely to have professional connections to government and lawmakers, more education, and a better understanding of how to make their voices heard. And the wealthy are more likely to have business interests that can be affected— either positively or negatively—by the actions of lawmakers, so they engage with politicians to protect their wealth.

Politicians themselves tend to be rich. In 2014 the 535 members of Congress (the US Senate and the US House of Representatives) had a collective net worth of at least $2.1 billion. At least one-third of them were millionaires. And their median net worth—about $450,000—was firmly within the top 10 percent of the nation. Wealthy politicians sometimes vote in favor of their own self-interests.

Incoming members of Congress stand on the steps of the Capitol in Washington, DC, in November 2016. Running for public office is extremely expensive, and many elected officials are wealthy.

And the opinions, concerns, and problems of the well-to-do are more familiar to them. They may be unaware of the problems that face the poor and middle class.

A person planning to run for political office has to have or be able to raise a lot of money. Political campaigns are expensive. Candidates and their supporters pay for advertisements on television, radio, and the Internet. Travel is another huge expense. Candidates visit cities around the state or nation to shake hands, pose for photos, and make speeches. They hire big staffs, including campaign managers, advisers, speechwriters, fund-raisers, photographers, and pollsters. They rent offices and purchase computers and other equipment and supplies. They hire staff to recruit, organize, and manage volunteers. Candidates, political parties, and independent interest groups spent nearly $7 billion on the 2016 presidential and congressional elections. About $2.7 billion of that money went to the presidential election.

Spending a lot of money doesn't always guarantee a win, but it has a significant impact. In the 2014 congressional elections, for example, the candidate who spent the most money won in 94 percent of the US House of Representative races and in 82 percent of US Senate races. In every presidential race between 1964 and 2012, the candidate who raised the most money also won the presidency.

Where does all this money come from? The federal government offers public money to presidential candidates, as long as they adhere to certain spending limits. But many candidates reject public financing—and spending limits—and instead look to donations, both large and small, to fund their campaigns. The money comes from citizens, corporations, and unions.

The Federal Election Commission (FEC) is responsible for making sure that elections in the United States are fair. It does so by strictly limiting how much money individuals and groups, such as corporations and unions, can give to political candidates and political parties. These restrictions were established to make sure that the wealthy did not use their money to unfairly influence elections. However, in a 2010 Supreme Court case called *Citizens United v. FEC*, the Supreme Court ruled that wealthy groups and individuals can spend as much money as they like on political advertising, as long as they do not give the money directly to candidates or parties. Instead, individuals, corporations, and unions can pool their money and pay for ads that support candidates or that attack their political opponents. They can do so as long as they do not coordinate directly with a candidate's campaign. The court said that spending money on political messages is a form of speech. The US Constitution guarantees the right to free speech and so, the court ruled, limits on campaign spending are unconstitutional. The ruling was controversial, and four of the nine Supreme Court justices disagreed with the majority opinion. They believed that the ruling opened the door for wealthy individuals, unions, and corporations to have far too much influence over American politics.

Since the ruling, wealthy groups and individuals have been pouring great amounts of money into political action committees (PACs) and super PACS. These organizations take in funds from donors and use them to defeat or support particular political candidates. After *Citizens United*, between 2010 and 2015, super PACs spent nearly $1 billion on federal elections. Nearly 60 percent of that money came from just 195 donors. That means wealthy people are paying hundreds of thousands and sometimes millions of dollars to influence campaigns.

LOBBYISTS HAVE LOUD VOICES

As long as there have been lawmakers, there have been people trying to influence them. Companies, trade associations, nonprofit organizations, and other groups hire lobbyists to represent their points of view to elected officials and to try to influence the types of decisions they make. In 2016 more than 11,143 lobbyists worked in Washington, DC—that's more than twenty lobbyists for each member of Congress. Many lobbyists have offices on K Street, which is famous for its lobbyists the same way Wall Street is famous for its bankers.

Lobbyists meet with politicians and try to convince them to pass (or not pass) laws and regulations that affect their clients. Lobbyists sometimes write bills that would benefit a client and try to convince lawmakers to introduce those bills into Congress. Lobbyists know a lot about the political process. Many politicians and government officials become lobbyists after they leave office. They use their political expertise and connections to influence lawmakers. And they make a lot of money. Well-connected lobbyists can earn more than $500,000 a year.

Any group can hire a lobbyist. Large institutions, such as universities and hospitals, often hire lobbyists. So do identity groups, which represent the interests of particular ethnic and religious

After former senators John Breaux (*left*) and Trent Lott (*center*) left political office, they joined a lobbying firm, Squire Patton Boggs. As lobbyists, Breaux and Lott can use their insider connections to influence members of Congress.

communities, the elderly, women, lesbian, gay, bisexual, transgender, and queer/questioning (LGBTQ) peoples, and others. Groups that advocate for the environment, gun rights or gun control, consumer protections, civil liberties, and other causes also hire lobbyists.

Some US state and local governments hire lobbyists to represent their interests at the national level. Even foreign governments and corporations hire lobbyists to represent them in Washington. That's because the policies of the United States, the world's largest superpower, have a huge impact on the rest of the world.

Because lobbyists are expensive, wealthy companies are more likely to hire them than are nonprofit organizations, which have small budgets. More than half of the lobbying organizations in Washington represent business interests. Less than 5 percent focus on public interest causes such as environmental protections, and about 4 percent focus on identity groups. Less than 1 percent of these organizations are specifically aimed at helping the poor.

The scale is even more unbalanced in dollars spent. Corporations and other business interests have vastly more money to spend on lobbying than groups of ordinary citizens. The biggest spenders and the amounts spent in 2015 are these:

- the health-care sector ($510 million)
- the finance, insurance, and real estate sectors ($486 million)
- oil, gas, coal, and other resource extraction interests ($326 million)
- transportation ($223 million)
- other assorted business interests ($510 million)

In comparison, unions spent $46 million on lobbying. Millions of nonunionized workers, on the other hand, had no lobbyists to represent their interests.

WHAT DOES POLITICAL INFLUENCE BUY?

Between lobbying and political donations, corporations spend huge amounts of money on politics. The two hundred companies that spent the most on political activities from 2007 to 2012 paid out a combined $5.8 billion. What does all that money buy?

One payoff for big spenders is government contracts. The US government buys many products, from food for schoolchildren to computers for government offices and expensive military equipment. It signs contracts with private businesses to supply these goods. Not by accident, these contracts often go to companies that make big campaign donations and spend large sums on lobbying. Between 2007 and 2012, government contracts for goods and services totaled a little more than $3 trillion. One-third of that money went to the top two hundred corporate political spenders. Weapons manufacturer Boeing, for example, spent a combined $104 million on campaign contributions

President Donald Trump emerges from an Air Force One presidential airplane built by Boeing. Boeing spends millions of dollars on campaign contributions and lobbying each year. It also receives rich government contracts to build vehicles and military equipment.

to and lobbying of lawmakers from 2007 to 2013. During that period, Boeing received more than $187 billion in government contracts to provide the Department of Defense (DOD) with a range of goods, including satellites and missiles. The exchange was not a documented transaction—the government and Boeing did not sign an agreement trading campaign contributions for military contracts. But when approving the contracts, members of Congress were fully aware of the company's generous contributions to their campaigns and viewed the company in a favorable light. Pressure from Boeing's lobbyists also convinced lawmakers to approve the contracts.

The US government also leases parcels of federal land to energy companies. With the leases, the companies then have the right to extract oil, natural gas, and coal from these lands. These resources are extremely valuable, and companies will sell them for huge profits. Here too companies that spend big money on lobbying lawmakers and campaign contributions are more likely to win energy leases than those that spend less or don't spend at all.

One of the most valuable prizes the government gives to rich corporations is tax breaks. According to federal law, the corporate tax rate is 35 percent. That means, in theory, that the Internal Revenue Service takes 35 percent of the profits that corporations amass each year. However, most corporations pay far less because of tax loopholes—provisions in tax laws that allow corporations to reduce their tax payments for a wide range of reasons.

Tax loopholes make a huge difference. Every year from 2008 to 2010, 288 Fortune 500 companies (the 500 highest-earning US

LOBBYING'S BIG SPENDERS ◄-------------

Lobbying groups in the United States spend millions of dollars every year to convince lawmakers to pass laws that favor certain groups. This list shows the top ten lobbying groups, according to how much they spent in 2016. Four of the ten are in the health-care industry, which is a huge sector of the US economy, especially as the population ages.

Organization	Millions spent
US Chamber of Commerce (business association)	$79.2
National Association of Realtors	$45.3
Blue Cross Blue Shield (medical insurance association)	$19.1
American Hospital Association	$15.5
American Medical Association	$15.3
Pharmaceutical Research and Manufacturers of America	$14.7
Boeing Company (airplane and weapons manufacturer)	$12.9
AT&T (communications company)	$12.7
National Association of Broadcasters	$12.1
Google (Internet services company)	$11.9

> Highly paid lobbyists pressure congressional members to change the tax code (tax laws) to benefit their clients. . . . It's not just corporations that get big tax breaks. Wealthy citizens get them too.

companies, ranked each year by *Fortune* magazine) made a profit. On average, these corporations paid only 19.4 percent in taxes on those profits. One-third of the corporations paid less than 10 percent. And 26 of the corporations paid no federal taxes at all during the two-year period. How is this possible? The answer goes back to lobbying and campaign funding. Highly paid lobbyists pressure congressional members to change the tax code (tax laws) to benefit their clients. And when those clients have also contributed hundreds of thousands of dollars (or more) to help them get elected, congressional members often comply. As an example, Congress approved a provision in the tax code, Section 833, that saves the health insurance company Blue Cross Blue Shield an estimated $1 billion a year. The company was also the third-highest spender on lobbying in 2016. Congressional representatives say yes to these kinds of deals for fear that if they say no, companies will stop contributing money to their campaigns. And without the money, most lawmakers couldn't run for office.

It's not just corporations that get big tax breaks. Wealthy citizens get them too. Jeffery A. Winters, a political scientist at Northwestern University in Illinois, told the *New York Times* that the richest people in the United States "literally pay millions of dollars" to experts who help them navigate the complex US tax system. These experts help the ultrawealthy each "save in the tens or hundreds of millions in taxes."

Fast-food workers would benefit from a higher minimum wage. But in 2014, when the US Senate considered a bill that would raise the wage from $7.25 to $10.10 per hour, business associations strongly disagreed. They lobbied senators to vote against the bill, and it failed to pass.

CONTROL OVER THE RULE BOOK

Because of their political clout, rich people help write the rules of the game. And they tend to support rules that favor their own interests instead of the interests of workers, consumers, and the environment.

Take, for example, the federal minimum wage, which in 2009 was $7.25 an hour. In April 2014, the US Senate voted on a bill to raise the minimum wage to $10.10, a move that would have benefited more than 20.6 million Americans. Shortly before the vote, members of Congress received a letter from twenty trade associations, including the US Chamber of Commerce, the National Restaurant Association, and the National Federation of Independent Business. The letter said, "Raising the minimum wage will be detrimental to job creation and low-skilled workers trying to get started on the economic ladder." The associations claimed that paying workers more would greatly decrease profits, so that businesses, especially small businesses, would be unable to hire as many workers as they needed. This would hurt workers, the businesses argued, since they would be better off with low-paying jobs than no jobs at all. By mentioning people "just getting started on the economic ladder," the letter implied that minimum wage jobs are usually held by young people who will soon move up into higher-paid positions.

MARGARET'S LIFE ON MINIMUM WAGE ◄-------

Margaret is a single mom with three children. She wakes at 6:00 a.m. every morning and exercises for half an hour before she gets her children ready for school. Her daughters are six and seven. After putting them on the school bus, Margaret takes her son, who is four, to preschool. She then goes to a job resource center to do homework for her high school equivalency degree (GED). She uses a computer at the center because she does not have one of her own. Then she picks up her son from preschool, feeds him lunch, and sets him down for a nap. About an hour later, she takes him to day care so she can get to her job at a fast-food restaurant by 2:00 p.m. She works there until 12:30 or 1:00 in the morning. Meanwhile, her brother picks up her daughters from school and they stay with him until Margaret picks them up after work. She takes them home, goes to bed, and does it all over again the next day. The schedule is grueling, and adding to the stress, Margaret's fast-food job doesn't pay enough to support her and her kids. So she must rely on help from others. She says,

> I don't mind getting hand-me-downs. But it feels good when I can buy my babies what they need—shoes, clothes, underwear. Not even what they want, just what they need. My son is growing out of his shoes, and so the daycare provider went out and bought my son some shoes. I appreciate what she's doing, but as a mother, I feel bad that I'm not able to buy my kids a pair of shoes when they need it. My girls have four pairs of shoes that they share.

This is true to some extent. About half of minimum wage workers are under the age of twenty-five. However, many older workers, including those with families to support, also depend on minimum wage jobs. Altogether, the twenty groups that sent the letter had spent $91 million on overall lobbying efforts the previous year. And the bill did not pass.

The political influence of the affluent does not just reproduce inequality. It also increases it. By giving the wealthy tax breaks, government contracts, and other benefits while keeping minimum wages low, the government helps the rich get even richer while everyone else gets poorer. Many Americans have become angry and resentful. They recognize that their government is not protecting their interests and economic well-being, nor is it listening to their concerns.

CHAPTER SIX

WHAT CAN BE DONE?

Is economic inequality normal and healthy for a society? Some experts say it is. They argue that successful businesses and individuals deserve to be rewarded with great profits and wealth. Taking money away from them, through taxes and other means, is unfair, they say, as are government regulations that constrain business operations. Furthermore, taking money from the very rich discourages innovation—entrepreneurs will be less motivated to start a new business or invent the next big thing if the government taxes the fortune that comes from that achievement. Inequality

Alexis Lewis was just thirteen when she invented and 3-D printed a lightweight emergency kit for people trapped in fires. Some experts say that heavily taxing entrepreneurs such as Lewis discourages their creative spirit.

encourages people to work hard, according to this argument, and when people work hard, businesses and their employees do well and the economy thrives.

Others say that economic inequality is unhealthy for a society, especially if the gap between rich and poor is too big. They argue that Americans can and should take steps to reduce inequality to reclaim the American Dream. How might that be done?

REDISTRIBUTION

Many proposed solutions rely on government action. For example, Thomas Piketty and other economists say that the US government could redistribute money. Specifically, it could take money from top earners by taxing them heavily and distribute that money equally throughout the rest of the population. Each adult and child would get a basic income with no strings attached. This money would provide for the essentials of life—food, clothing, and shelter—and by spending it, citizens would boost the economy. And citizens could supplement the basic income with earnings from jobs.

A variation on the basic income, proposed by British economist Anthony Atkinson, is a participatory income. Basic income guarantees an income for all. A participatory income comes with the condition that to earn this money, a person must perform a socially useful activity. This could be volunteer work, going to school, caring for children, or helping a disabled or elderly relative. Atkinson proposes that each person's participatory income equal about one-quarter of the nation's median income. This income would help poor people pay for basic needs but would not discourage them from also seeking paid work or pursuing business ideas.

Another idea is that the government should invest a small amount of money on behalf of each newborn child. The money would earn interest over time, tax-free. At the age of eighteen, a child would claim the money invested on his or her behalf and use it to pay for college or to start a new business. Often young people can't get loans to start businesses because they lack collateral—something of value, such as a house, that the lending bank can take if a loan is not repaid. With a government investment program, more young Americans could start businesses and hire workers. The results would benefit the economy.

Such dramatic redistributive programs are unlikely to take off in the United States anytime soon. Many Americans believe that those who earn money deserve that money, while those who do not or cannot earn money are seen as less worthy. Many Americans also have a deep and historic distrust of government and generally believe that government should allow individuals a great deal of freedom. So the idea of government controlling the distribution of wealth—especially if it means taking money from one person and giving it to another—is not popular in the United States.

THE COST OF HEALTH CARE

Americans pay significantly more for health care than people in any other nation. Experts say that the cost is higher because the US government allows private businesses to run the show. It does not step in to regulate health-care prices as the governments of other nations do. Office visits are three times more expensive in the United States than they are in Canada. Prescription drugs cost up to ten times more in the United States than they do in the United Kingdom or Germany. Most Americans also buy individual or employee-sponsored health insurance plans. Under such plans, insurance companies pay a portion of a policyholder's medical bills. Insurance plans allow patients to receive medical treatments costing tens or even hundreds of thousands of dollars without having to pay all the bills themselves. But insurance plans themselves are extremely expensive, since insurance companies must make a profit to pay their executives and other workers, and to pay dividends (a portion of their profits) to shareholders.

DROWNING IN DEBT

Debt is not always a bad thing. Borrowing money enables consumers to buy expensive items that might be unobtainable if the entire purchase price were required up front. Instead of paying all at once, buyers agree to make manageable payments spread out over many months or years. Such a system lets even low-income consumers buy high-ticket items, such as houses and cars. Borrowing money and paying it back on time also enables a consumer to build a strong credit rating. When lenders see that a potential borrower consistently pays back his or her loans, they are more willing to make additional loans to that person.

But borrowers who can't keep up with debt payments can face financial ruin. A lender might repossess the house or car of someone who fails to make monthly payments. Lenders can even go to court and get permission to take a portion of a worker's wages to pay off outstanding debt. Many companies sell outstanding debts to collection agencies for a low price, hoping to recoup some of their losses. The agencies hound debtors, threatening them with lawsuits in an attempt to collect as much of the original debt as possible.

In the twenty-first century, with the cost of living increasing faster than wages, many Americans are drowning in debt. US household debt increased by 11 percent between 2006 and 2016. In 2016, 43 percent of Americans with student loan debt were behind on their payments.

DEBT RELIEF

Those who can't pay their debts have some options for relief. For example, a lender might agree to settle a debt for a reduced amount. Suppose a patient owes $10,000 in medical bills. The hospital could ask the patient to pay that money in small installments, over many years. But it might agree to settle that debt for a lump-sum payment of, say, $5,000. That way, the hospital gets at least some of the money it's owed and it doesn't have to hassle with tracking many years of small payments. For consumers who owe money to many different lenders, some businesses offer debt consolidation programs. Under such programs, the borrower takes out a new loan, uses the money to pay off the various lenders, and makes one easier-to-manage payment on the new loan.

Declaring bankruptcy can be a method of wiping out debt either partially or completely. It is a legal process governed by federal and state law. When consumers declare bankruptcy, they are legally entitled to pay only a portion of their outstanding debts or nothing at all. Declaring bankruptcy comes at a high cost, though. It can severely damage a person's credit rating, preventing him or her from taking out new loans for many years or allow borrowing only at very high interest rates.

Many students take out thousands of dollars in loans to pay for college and can't keep up with the payments afterward. But college graduates who enter certain professions can take advantage of loan forgiveness programs, offered by the federal government and other organizations. For instance, teachers, nurses, federal government employees, and those who work for social service organizations might qualify for loan forgiveness. Programs vary by profession, by number of years on the job, by lending organization, and by the terms of the loan.

One charity, Rolling Jubilee, buys debt from lenders and then forgives it rather than collecting it. As of February 2017, according to its website, Rolling Jubilee had raised more than $700,000 and forgiven almost $32 million in debt, focusing on student debt and medical debt.

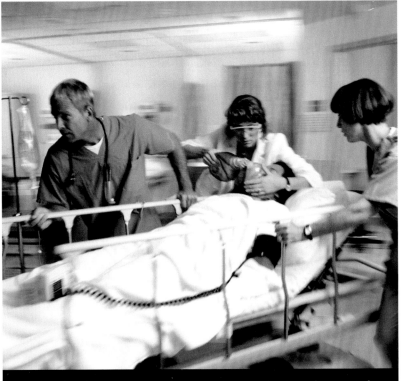

Health care in the United States is extremely expensive. To reduce costs for patients, some suggest a system in which the government pays everyone's medical bills.

The Affordable Care Act (ACA), signed into law in 2010, helps pay for the health insurance of millions of people who could not otherwise afford it. It also prevents insurance companies from refusing to provide policies to people who are already sick. Under the ACA, insurance companies must also pay for certain types of care, including yearly checkups and maternity care. The ACA is a popular government program, but many Republicans in Congress are trying to abolish the program.

In many countries, such as Canada, Australia, and most nations of Europe, insurance companies are not involved in the health-care system. The national government pays for all its citizens' health care. This kind of system ensures care for everyone, regardless of how much money people have. It also makes health care cheaper because the government negotiates directly with health-care providers for fair prices. No money for medical services is syphoned off to insurance companies and their shareholders. US consumers would likely realize enormous savings on medical bills if the United States switched to this type of health-care payment system.

INVESTING IN COMMUNITIES

Another way to address economic inequality is to make sure families have the support they need to raise children. For example, many European nations provide paid maternity and paternity leave—time off for new mothers and fathers. Some governments also offer a small payment to family members who do the work of raising young children and caring for elderly parents, a sick spouse, or disabled siblings. Without such payments, family members might have to deplete their life savings or lose wages to care for loved ones. Many experts say the United States would benefit from following this model.

Others argue that the federal, state, and local governments could put more money into public schools. This would help ensure that larger numbers of students get a good education with the best opportunity to succeed. The federal government could also expand programs that provide high-quality day care, preschool, mentoring, and tutoring to children. And if the government allotted more money for higher education, then vocational schools, community colleges, universities, and professional schools could lower tuition costs. Fewer students would end up with crippling debt.

Strong infrastructure, such as bridges and highways, is important for society. When roadways are in bad repair, traffic accidents increase. Infrastructure building and repair projects provide jobs for construction workers. Well-functioning public transit systems help

In the first decade of the twenty-first century, the states of Maryland and Virginia joined with the federal government to replace the Woodrow Wilson Memorial Bridge, which spans the Potomac River near Washington, DC. The governments spent $1.6 billion to build a new, larger bridge. The money paid for equipment, building materials, and construction workers' wages. All this government spending helped commuters and the local economy.

workers commute to jobs with less reliance on private cars. Facilities such as libraries and parks enrich communities. Many experts say that government should invest in such projects to strengthen society and the economy.

SHIFTING THE TAX BURDEN

Keep in mind that government projects, including child care, schools, and infrastructure, cost money—and that money ultimately comes from taxpayers. Many Americans want lower local, state, and federal taxes. But if governments don't collect much tax money, they can't provide services that benefit citizens.

Some conservative politicians call for lowering taxes so that citizens and businesses can keep more of their hard-earned money. But many public policy experts say that rather than lowering taxes, the government should change the way it taxes citizens. Such changes would still allow for helpful government services but would make taxes less burdensome to citizens.

Experts point out that some taxes affect the poor and middle classes more than they affect the rich. An example is sales taxes, which consumers pay when they purchase goods and services. Since poor and middle-class people must spend almost all the money they make to get by, they pay a large portion of their income in sales taxes. The rich, by contrast, save and invest much of their income, so sales taxes eat up a smaller percentage of the money they earn. Eliminating sales taxes would help decrease economic inequality.

In place of sales taxes, government could increase the tax rate on capital gains, a move that some believe would promote economic equality. Profits that individuals and businesses make when they buy stocks or property at one price and sell it at a higher price are called capital gains. In the United States, the federal government taxes capital gains at a lower rate than it taxes salary income. Capital gains are insignificant for most Americans. In 2012, for example, such earnings made up less than 1 percent of the total income of people making less than $200,000 a year. By contrast, capital gains made up more than half of the income of the nation's four hundred highest-income earners that year. Raising the tax on capital gains would not only provide more revenue to the federal government, but the money would come from those who could most afford it—the very rich.

The United States has a graduated income tax—the more you earn, the higher the percentage of your income is paid in taxes. A graduated income tax promotes equality by taxing the rich more heavily than the poor. Yet through tax loopholes, the extremely rich avoid much of the income tax they would otherwise have to pay. In 1993 the highest-earning taxpayers in the United States paid about 27 percent of their income in federal taxes. With more loopholes in place by 2012, the high earners paid less than 17 percent. Removing some of these loopholes would restore higher taxes on the wealthy, provide more revenue for the government, and help close the gap between rich and poor.

Removing loopholes in the corporate tax code could raise a great deal of revenue too. Two possible loopholes to close are deferrals and inversions. When US companies move some of their operations abroad, they pay taxes on those operations at the host country's tax rate (which is usually lower than US taxes). A company has to pay US taxes only on profits spent or deposited in banks in the United States. Known as tax deferral, this system encourages companies to move their operations overseas and to invest their profits there rather than at home. And the companies create jobs in other countries rather than in the United States.

Inversions occur when a large US company buys and merges with a smaller foreign company and benefits from foreign tax rates. For example, US-based Burger King bought Canadian restaurant Tim Hortons in 2014. The larger, merged company—Restaurant Brands International—could then file taxes in Canada, where taxes are lower. All the company's US corporate offices remain open, but it no longer pays US taxes.

LABOR UNITED

Unions have helped workers obtain fair pay and economic equality at various times in US history. In the 1950s, about 35 percent of US workers belonged to unions. Over the decades, however, companies have been very successful at crippling unions, and membership has declined significantly. By 2017 only about 10 percent of American workers belonged to unions. When unions have many dues-paying members, they have more money and more power. They can more effectively lobby politicians to pass laws that benefit workers. And when more industries are unionized, a greater percentage of US workers benefit. So increasing union membership and the number of unions overall is important in promoting economic equality.

By joining together in unions, workers can pressure their employers to provide higher pay and better working conditions. Here, striking Chicago teachers call for a more favorable employment contract and more state funding for Illinois schools.

Organizing workers into unions has never been easy. Many companies work diligently and with frightening tactics to keep workers from joining unions. For example, Wal-Mart employs 1.4 million Americans—a full 1 percent of the country's working population. But the only Wal-Mart employees to ever successfully join a union were ten meat cutters in Jacksonville, Texas. Their employment as union members did not last long. Within days of the meat cutters' vote to join the United Food and Commercial Workers in 2000, Wal-Mart announced that it would eliminate meat cutting in all its stores. That happened a few weeks later.

Company owners and executives believe that they will earn lower profits if employees unionize and demand higher wages. So they use a number of tactics to discourage unionization. Some companies require employees to listen to talks about the disadvantages of unions. Others put raises on hold during unionization campaigns. Others find excuses to fire union leaders.

In the face of such attacks, unions are using creative strategies to fight for US workers. To combat negative messages about unions, members are reaching out to local communities using social media and face-to-face communication. Some unions are using similar tactics to boost their own membership numbers. Others are sponsoring apprentice and leadership programs to help members boost their professional skills. Many unions ally themselves with other community organizations, such as charities, social justice organizations, and schools, as well as with unions in other sectors. And unions are still fighting the old-fashioned way, using strikes and demonstrations to pressure bosses into meeting their demands for fair pay and better working conditions.

REGULATIONS

Some politicians, particularly those in the Republican Party, argue that government regulations kill jobs because they can make it more costly to do business, cut into profits, and prevent companies from hiring additional workers. But others say that the disadvantages of regulations must be weighed against the benefits. For example, government regulations can ensure that medicines, foods, and other products are safe and effective. Regulations protect workers and the environment and can help rein in the power of big corporations.

Many public policy experts say that more and tighter government regulations—of both politics and business—would help reduce economic inequality in the United States. For example, stricter limits on campaign spending could help level the playing field so that Americans of lower income levels would have a fairer shot at political power. However, this change would require the Supreme Court to reverse its *Citizens United* decision, which said in 2010 that it is unconstitutional to limit the amount of money spent on political advertising. Congress could also approve and set aside more money for public campaign funding, so that candidates without personal wealth or wealthy connections could afford to run for political office.

Many Americans want to see greater restrictions on lobbying. After they leave office, lawmakers often become corporate lobbyists. Public officials are legally required to wait one year (for congressional representatives), two years (for senators), or five years (for executive branch officials) after leaving office before becoming lobbyists. Many officials call themselves consultants, or strategic advisers instead of lobbyists to get around this rule. And politicians often appoint wealthy corporate executives to powerful government positions. These close connections among lawmakers, lobbyists, and corporate leaders enhance the political power of big money in the United States. To halt this trend, Congress could lengthen the waiting periods and close some of the loopholes that allow former government officials to work as lobbyists without calling themselves lobbyists.

Legal scholars say that regulations to more strictly control the banking and financial industries might help prevent another financial crisis like that of 2008. President Barack Obama put many new regulations in place during his two terms in office (2008–2016). For instance, the Volcker Rule, which went into effect in 2014, prohibits banks from making the kinds of risky investments that contributed to the 2008 crisis. The administration of President Donald J. Trump (who took office in 2017) would like to abolish many of these rules, since banks can't make as much money if they follow them.

Finally, besides more regulations, many activists support a higher federal minimum wage. They say this would decrease inequality by putting more money in the pockets of low-wage workers, who would then spend that money and boost the economy. Higher wages would also allow workers to set aside some money into savings, which could be used in retirement or to cover bills during an emergency.

WHAT CAN BE DONE?

CITIZEN ACTION

What can average Americans do to reduce economic inequality? One approach is to get political. In 2011 protesters set up camp in Zuccotti Park in New York's financial district. Calling themselves Occupy Wall Street, the protesters were determined to awaken the public to economic inequality. They popularized the terms "the 99 percent" and "the 1 percent." With savvy media messaging, they were successful at attracting Americans to their movement. The movement quickly spread to cities around the United States and the world. The problem of economic inequality was a central topic of debate in the presidential elections of 2012 and 2016.

Besides joining protest movements, Americans can take other forms of political action. Even before you turn eighteen and are old enough to vote, you can make your voice heard. Call, e-mail, or message your political representatives and let them know your opinions. Lawmakers sometimes hold town hall meetings, where constituents can voice their concerns. Show up at those meetings and participate. It's a great way to be heard. Volunteer to work for candidates and causes you believe in. Share and discuss information with friends, neighbors, and students at your school. Read reputable newspapers and magazines and follow authoritative social media to learn about the issues—informed voters make better choices. Encourage your peers, parents, and other adults to vote. If you have a driver's license and a car and know someone who can't get to the polls, offer a ride.

Participate locally as well as nationally. It's sometimes easier to change laws on the neighborhood, city, or state level than on the national level. For example, the federal minimum wage has remained the same since 2009 (at $7.25 an hour). Yet twenty-nine states have a higher minimum wage. In some of these states, the minimum wage increases automatically as inflation rises. Some cities where the cost of living is particularly high, including New York, Seattle, and

The Fight for $15 is a campaign to raise the minimum wage to $15 per hour. Many experts say that a higher minimum wage would help reduce economic inequality.

Washington, DC, have raised their minimum wages to $15 an hour. These victories for workers came about because concerned citizens fought to increase the minimum wage. In some places, citizens voted to approve the increases. In others, lawmakers voted for the increases.

You can start even closer to home—at your school. Get involved in student government. Talk to kids about what matters to them. See if you can work together to make improvements in your school. For example, kids at Austin High School in Austin, Texas, wanted an automatic door so kids in wheelchairs could easily enter the school. They worked together to raise money, and bingo, they got the door.

WHAT CAN BE DONE?

By patronizing local cafés and other small businesses, residents help keep money in their own communities.

VOTE WITH YOUR DOLLARS

Big corporations and small businesses alike make their money the same way: by selling goods and services to consumers. So you, as a consumer, have power. Be aware of where you spend your money. When you buy a cup of coffee at an independent café rather than Starbucks or pick out a birthday gift at a quirky local boutique rather than ordering something from Amazon, you are supporting your local community rather than a giant corporation. Supporting local businesses creates a healthy local economy. When they succeed and are able to hire more workers, those workers will likely come from your community. And local businesses often sponsor youth sports teams, donate to local charities, and buy equipment and services from other local businesses.

Many people assume that prices are always higher at small shops than at large chain stores. This is not always true. Nor do the big-box stores necessarily have better selections. They sell many different types of goods, but the range of products within a given category may be very limited. Buyers might find something more interesting or unusual at a small shop. Customer service is also likely to be better in a small shop. People who run small businesses are often more knowledgeable and passionate about what they are selling than employees at chain stores. And they are more likely to remember and look out for the needs of their customers.

Local businesses give a community character and vitality. They also funnel profits and jobs away from big corporations and into the hands of the 99 percent. By giving small local businesses your dollars, you also help reduce economic inequality.

NEW BUSINESS MODELS

Some entrepreneurs have set out to reduce economic inequality on a small scale—at the local level and within individual businesses. About 29.7 million Americans live in food deserts, or low-income neighborhoods where the nearest grocery store is more than 1 mile (1.6 km) away. Without nearby grocery stores, residents can't easily get fresh and healthy foods. Their only easy options are fast-food chains, with heavily processed, nutritionally poor food. Two former Wall Street brokers, Sam Polk and David Foster, founded a store called Everytable, where poor residents of South Los Angeles can get delicious, healthy takeout food. Everytable also has a store for residents in a wealthy neighborhood in downtown LA. In a central kitchen, two talented chefs make dishes such as Jamaican jerk chicken and Caesar salad. The food is packaged into containers that can be heated in microwave ovens at the store or taken home.

In the South LA location, where the main competitors are fast-food chains, the meals sell for about four dollars each. But in the downtown neighborhood, where the competition consists of upscale stores such as Whole Foods, the meals sell for about eight dollars apiece. Foster explains, "Each store is designed to be individually profitable. At $4 per meal in South LA, we're not making much money from each meal sold. But if we get enough people to come out—and we're already seeing great traction—it will actually be profitable. The location downtown will also be profitable. So together they're part of this company that's working to improve access [to healthy food]. The higher-price location will help fund the growth of new locations in both markets."

Variations on this theme are pay-what-you-can restaurants, which serve good food in a pleasant atmosphere to those who would otherwise not be able to afford it. Some provide a bill with a suggested price and allow patrons to pay whatever amount they can afford. Some ask patrons who cannot pay in money to help out with work. Some charge well-off customers extra money, using it to provide a free dinner for a needy person. Mariana Chilton, founder of Philadelphia's EAT Café, told the *Washington Post*, "I couldn't stand the idea that you have these gorgeous restaurants with nice food, and there are families who are struggling who could never tap into that. I wanted to make a place where families could come experience some joy."

AN EXPERIMENT IN EQUALITY

In 2000 Dan Price was a sixteen-year-old musician, playing in coffee shops with his rock band. He noticed that the shops got a raw deal from credit card–processing companies. They paid exorbitant fees on each transaction. Price developed a business that provided the service at a lower cost. In 2004 he went into partnership with his older brother, Lucas. By the time Dan Price was in his early thirties, Seattle-based Gravity Payments was a success. It brought in more than $13 million in revenue in 2013. As company CEO, Price took home an annual salary of more than $1 million.

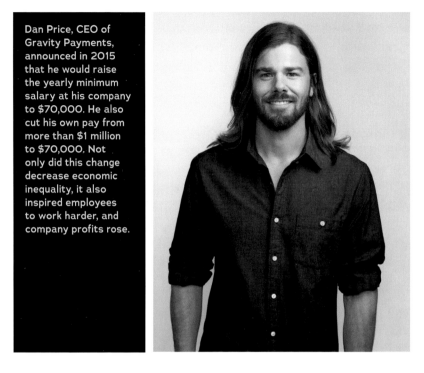

Dan Price, CEO of Gravity Payments, announced in 2015 that he would raise the yearly minimum salary at his company to $70,000. He also cut his own pay from more than $1 million to $70,000. Not only did this change decrease economic inequality, it also inspired employees to work harder, and company profits rose.

A conversation with a low-paid employee made Price think about the inequality within his own company. The worker felt "ripped off" because he made so much less than Price while working just as hard. So Price decided to give his employees a 20 percent pay raise. Productivity increased, and the company's profits rose just as much as they had in the previous year, even with the increase in salaries. The same thing happened the next year—20 percent raises and 30 to 40 percent increases in productivity. Finally, inspired by the struggles of a smart, hardworking friend who could hardly pay her rent, Price decided to make a more radical change.

He had read a study co-authored by psychologist Daniel Kahneman and economist Angus Eaton, both Nobel Prize winners, about the relationship between money and happiness. The study showed that making more money does make people happier—up until

WHAT CAN BE DONE?

an annual salary of about $75,000. Making more than $75,000 a year does not significantly increase happiness, according to the study. So Price took a drastic pay cut to $70,000 per year and raised every employee's salary to the same $70,000 per year. He told *Inc.* magazine, "Most people live paycheck to paycheck. So how come I need 10 years of living expenses set aside and you don't? That doesn't make any sense. Having to depend on modest pay is not a bad thing. It will help me stay focused."

The company's $70,000 minimum salary attracted a huge amount of attention, inspired other companies to also raise wages, and brought new customers and new talent to Gravity Payments. One new employee is former Yahoo executive Tammi Kroll, who was so inspired by Price's business model that she came to work for Gravity at an 80 percent pay cut. "I spent many years chasing the money," she said. "Now I'm looking for something fun and meaningful."

A NEW GREAT PROSPERITY

The United States has known periods of economic equality— primarily in the decades following World War II. Many activists feel that economic equality can again become a reality in the United States. And stories such as Dan Price's, Sam Polk and David Foster's, and Mariana Chilton's show that individuals can make a difference. Individual decisions, group action, and government policy can impact the way money is distributed in society. The political and economic forces that sustain and increase inequality are powerful, and movement toward equality will not come on its own. It will take time, effort, and dedication by concerned Americans to make it happen. Former president Barack Obama stressed this in a speech to high school students in Kansas. He said,

This isn't just another political debate. This is the defining issue of our time. This is a make or break moment for the middle class, and all those who are fighting to get into the middle class. At stake is whether this will be a country where working people can earn enough to raise a family, build a modest savings, own a home, and secure their retirement. . . . I'm here to reaffirm my deep conviction that we are greater together than we are on our own. I believe that this country succeeds when everyone gets a fair shot, when everyone does their fair share, and when everyone plays by the same rules. Those aren't Democratic or Republican values; 1% values or 99% values. They're American values, and we have to reclaim them.

—President Barack Obama, 2011

ACKNOWLEDGMENTS

I thank Dr. Michael L. Frazer, lecturer in political and social theory at the University of East Anglia, for being my expert consultant. He helped me find sources, double-checked my facts and the logic of my arguments, and helped clean up my prose. I also thank Michael for insisting that this project was important and that I could do it, for taking on extra household chores when I needed to get writing done, and for being the most supportive husband imaginable. I love you, babe.

Many of Michael's friends and colleagues provided useful information about sources and important points to cover. Thank you to the political theory community; you are a lovely group of smart and interesting people. I would also like to thank Ragan O'Malley for giving me a school librarian's perspective on what would be useful in a book on this topic.

A huge thanks to Domenica Di Piazza, whose enthusiasm and advocacy made this project possible. I'm so grateful that you gave me this chance! Peg Goldstein was the most helpful editor imaginable, honing in on every instance where I was vague, left things implicit that needed to be stated outright, or let jargon creep in without defining it. This book would not be half as clear without her constant injunctions to "Explain! Define! Explain!" And thanks as well to infographics designer Laura Westlund and cover designer Kimberly Morales.

I must also thank my mother for always believing in me, my writing friends for helping me become a better writer, my brothers and sisters-in-law for being smart and awesome, my father for his passion for social justice, and my wonderful in-laws for hosting me at the conference where this whole thing got started. Finally, I would like to thank my son, Oren, for inspiring me with his happiness. Your enthusiasm for life brightens my every day.

SOURCE NOTES

14 "Great Depression and World War II, 1929–1945," Library of Congress, accessed May 29, 2017, http://www.loc.gov/teachers/classroommaterials/presentationsandactivities/presentations/timeline/depwwii/newdeal/.

53 Dominica Lim, "'I Feel Rich When I Have Food.' Stories from the War on Poverty," *Aljazeera America*, January 14, 2014, http://america.aljazeera.com/articles/2014/1/15/stories-from-thewaronpoverty.html.

59 Tina Griego, "How I Got Out of Poverty: 'I Don't Like to Think of Myself as an Outlier,'" *Washington Post*, October 28, 2014, https://www.washingtonpost.com/news/storyline/wp/2014/10/28/how-i-got-out/.

62 Robert Putnam, *Our Kids: The American Dream in Crisis* (New York: Simon and Schuster, 2015), 103.

62 American Academy of Pediatrics, "Poverty Threatens Health of US Children," *Science Daily*, May 4, 2013, https://www.sciencedaily.com/releases/2013/05/130504163257.htm

66 "The Carolina Abecedarian Project," Frank Porter Graham Child Development Institute, accessed May 16, 2016, http://abc.fpg.unc.edu/design-and-innovative-curriculum.

72 Veronica Hill, "$33,000 in Debt," *Huffington Post*, February 21, 2011, http://www.huffingtonpost.com/veronica-hill/debt-still-unavoidable-ev_b_825569.html.

75 Abraham Lincoln, "The Gettysburg Address," Abraham Lincoln Online, May 29, 2017.

90 Noam Scheiber and Patricia Cohen, "For the Wealthiest, a Private Tax System That Saves Them Billions," *New York Times*, December 29, 2015, https://www.nytimes.com/2015/12/30/business/economy/for-the-wealthiest-private-tax-system-saves-them-billions.html.

91 Robbie Feinberg, "The Money against the Minimum Wage," *OpenSecrets.org*, April 4, 2014, https://www.opensecrets.org/news/2014/04/the-political-money-against-the-min/.

92 Jill Filipovic, "What It's Like to Raise 3 Kids on $7.50 an Hour," *Cosmopolitan*, November 26, 2014, http://www.cosmopolitan.com/politics/news/a33665/what-its-like-to-live-on-minimum-wage/.

112 "One Restaurant's Recipe for Social Good: Same Meals, Different Prices," *NPR*, September 2, 2016, http://www.npr.org/sections/thesalt/2016/09/02/492240882/one-restaurants-recipe-for-social-good-same-meals-different-prices.

112 Maura Judkis, "'There's a Dignity to This Place': Inside the World of Pay-What -You-Can Restaurants," *Washington Post*, January 23, 2017, https://www .washingtonpost.com/lifestyle/food/inside-the-world-of-pay-what-you-can -restaurants-which-are-redefining-charity/2017/01/23/4b7b588e-d45e-11e6 -945a-76f69a399dd5_story.html?utm_term=.d339fbabc3ce.

113 Paul Keegan, "Here's What Really Happened at That Company That Set a $70,000 Minimum Wage," *Inc.*, accessed November 17, 2015, http://www.inc .com/magazine/201511/paul-keegan/does-more-pay-mean-more-growth.html.

114 Ibid.

114 Ibid.

115 Adam Clark Estes, "Obama's Income Inequality Speech, *Atlantic*, December 6, 2011, https://www.theatlantic.com/politics/archive/2011/12/obamas-income -inequality-speech/334664/.

GLOSSARY

absolute upward mobility: obtaining a higher income and level of education than one's parents obtained (adjusted for inflation). Social scientists look at absolute upward mobility to assess whether citizens in general are getting richer and better educated.

automation: the use of robots, computers, and other machines to do jobs once done by humans. Many US workers, particularly factory workers, have lost their jobs to automation.

capital gains: money made by selling investments, such as stocks or property. The US government taxes capital gains at a lower rate than it taxes workers' income. Most of those who earn capital gains are very wealthy, and some public policy experts and politicians propose raising taxes on capital gains to make the rich pay their fair share of taxes.

capitalism: an economic system in which privately owned businesses provide goods and services, with little government interference. The United States has a primarily capitalist economy.

credit: a provision of money, goods, or services with the expectation of future repayment. When consumers or businesses buy something on credit, they are borrowing money to be paid back later plus interest.

economic bubble: the rapid rise of an asset's price, followed by a sudden price decrease. US house prices went through an economic bubble in the first decade of the twenty-first century.

Gini index: a measure of inequality in which 0 represents perfect equality (everyone has the same amount) and 100 represents perfect inequality (one person has everything and everyone else has nothing). The United States has a Gini index score of 41, a high score when compared to other industrialized nations.

gross domestic product (GDP): the monetary value of all goods and services produced in a country within a certain period of time (often a year)

inflation: a general increase in the prices for goods and services. When economists compare wages and other costs from one period to another (for example, comparing a bank teller's salary in 1970 to a bank teller's salary in 2010), they must adjust for inflation.

interest: a fee that one pays for borrowing money, usually a percentage of the borrowed amount. Low interest rates encourage individuals and businesses to borrow money.

labor force: everyone aged sixteen and over who is either employed or actively looking for work

lobbyist: someone who tries to influence legislators to vote a certain way on a bill. Businesses and other organizations hire lobbyists to push for laws that benefit their interests.

mean: a value that equals the sum of a group of numbers divided by how many numbers there are

median: the middle value in an ordered list of values

minimum wage: the lowest hourly wage that a worker can be paid according to federal, state, or city law. In 2017 the federal minimum wage was $7.25, but many states and cities had higher minimum wages.

mortgage: a loan that enables someone to buy a home, farm, or other piece of property. If a mortgage is not repaid, the lender can take the property, or foreclose.

net worth: the total value of a family's or individual's assets (money and property) minus any debts; also called wealth

1 percent: those who are richer than 99 percent of their fellow Americans. In 2017 the 1 percent earned more than 20 percent of the income in the United States.

outsourcing: opening facilities and hiring workers in another country. Outsourcing saves US businesses money since most foreign workers will work for lower wages than Americans will.

productivity: the amount of goods and services an average worker can produce over a given period

relative mobility: the movement of children into a higher or lower social class than that of their parents. The United States has low relative mobility, so those who are born poor are likely to remain poor and those who are born rich are likely to remain rich.

socialism: an economic system in which the government is highly involved in providing goods and services to citizens. The United States has some Socialist programs, such as Medicare and Social Security.

stock: shares of ownership in a company. When a company that sells stock makes a profit, its shareholders get a portion of the money.

unemployment rate: the percentage of people aged sixteen and over who do not have a job and are actively looking for one

union: an organization of workers from a particular trade or industry that joins together to negotiate with business owners for higher wages and better working conditions. As union membership in the United States has decreased, economic inequality has increased.

wealth: the total value of a family's or individual's assets (money and property) minus debts; also called net worth

SELECTED BIBLIOGRAPHY

Anand, Anika, and Gus Lubin. "13 Foreclosure Horror Stories That Are Making Banker's Squirm." *Business Insider*, November 20, 2010. http://www .businessinsider.com/foreclosure-horror-stories-2010-11?IR=T#dan-smith-got -tricked-by-a-teaser-rate-3.

"Automation and Anxiety: Will Smarter Machines Cause Mass Unemployment?" *Economist*, June 25, 2016. http://www.economist.com/news/special-report /21700758-will-smarter-machines-cause-mass-unemployment-automation-and -anxiety.

Bartels, Larry M. *Unequal Democracy: The Political Economy in the New Gilded Age.* New York: Russell Sage Foundation/Princeton University Press, 2008.

Filipovic, Jill. "What It's Like to Raise 3 Kids on $7.50 an Hour." *Cosmopolitan*, November 26, 2014. http://www.cosmopolitan.com/politics/news/a33665/what -its-like-to-live-on-minimum-wage/.

Florida, Richard. "Understanding the Rise of the Global Super-Rich." *CityLab*, May 16, 2016. http://www.citylab.com/work/2016/05/world-billionaire-wealth-global -one-percent/482802/.

Gilens, Martin. *Affluence and Influence: Economic Inequality and Political Power in America*. Princeton, NJ: Princeton University Press/Russell Sage Foundation, 2012.

Griego, Tina. "How I Got Out of Poverty: 'I Don't Like to Think of Myself as an Outlier.'" *Washington Post*, October 28, 2014. https://www.washingtonpost.com /news/storyline/wp/2014/10/28/how-i-got-out/.

Hickel, Jason. "Global Inequality May Be Much Worse Than We Think." *Guardian* (US ed.), April 8, 2016. https://www.theguardian.com/global-development -professionals-network/2016/apr/08/global-inequality-may-be-much-worse-than -we-think.

Hill, Veronica. "$33,000 in Debt." *Huffington Post*. Last modified May 25, 2011. http://www.huffingtonpost.com/veronica-hill/debt-still-unavoidable -ev_b_825569.html.

Leonhardt, David. "The American Dream, Quantified at Last." *New York Times*, December 8, 2016. https://www.nytimes.com/2016/12/08/opinion/the-american -dream-quantified-at-last.html.

Lim, Dominica. "'I Feel Rich When I Have Food.' Stories from the War on Poverty." *Aljazeera America*, January 15, 2014. http://america.aljazeera.com /articles/2014/1/15/stories-from-thewaronpoverty.html.

Long, Heather. "U.S. Has Lost 5 Million Manufacturing Jobs since 2000." *CNN*, March 29, 2016. http://money.cnn.com/2016/03/29/news/economy/us -manufacturing-jobs/.

McElwee, Sean. "The Income Gap at the Polls." *Politico*, January 7, 2015. http://www .politico.com/magazine/story/2015/01/income-gap-at-the-polls-113997.

Noah, Timothy. *The Great Divergence: America's Growing Inequality Crisis and What We Can Do about It.* New York: Bloomsbury, 2012.

Piketty, Thomas. *Capital in the Twenty-First Century.* Translated by Arthur Goldhammer. Cambridge, MA: Belknap Press of Harvard University Press, 2014.

Polk, Sam. "For the Love of Money." *New York Times*, January 18, 2014. https://www .nytimes.com/2014/01/19/opinion/sunday/for-the-love-of-money.html.

Putnam, Robert D. *Our Kids: The American Dream in Crisis.* New York: Simon and Schuster, 2015.

Reich, Robert B. *Aftershock: The Next Economy and America's Future.* New York: Vintage Books, 2013.

Rich, Motoko, Amanda Cox, and Matthew Bloch. "Money, Race and Success: How Your School District Compares." *New York Times*, April 29, 2016. https://www .nytimes.com/interactive/2016/04/29/upshot/money-race-and-success-how-your -school-district-compares.html.

Rogers, Simon. "OECD Inequality Report: How Do Different Countries Compare?" *Guardian* (London), December 5, 2011. https://www.theguardian.com/news /datablog/2011/dec/05/oecd-ineqaulity-report-uk-us#data.

Samuelson, Robert J. "What's the Real Gender Pay Gap?" *Washington Post*, April 24, 2016. https://www.washingtonpost.com/opinions/whats-the-real-gender-pay-gap /2016/04/24/314a90ee-08a1-11e6-bdcb-0133da18418d_story.html?utm_term= .6f6d30fd74d0.

Schlozman, Kay Lehman, Sidney Verba, and Henry E. Brady. *The Unheavenly Chorus: Unequal Political Voice and the Broken Promise of American Democracy*. Princeton, NJ: Princeton University Press, 2012.

Schwartz, Larry. "35 Soul-Crushing Facts about American Income Inequality." *Salon*, July 15, 2015. http://www.salon.com/2015/07/15/35_soul_crushing_facts_about _american_income_inequality_partner/.

Shin, Laura. "The Racial Wealth Gap: Why a Typical White Household Has 16 Times the Wealth of a Black One." *Forbes*, March 26, 2015. https://www.forbes .com/sites/laurashin/2015/03/26/the-racial-wealth-gap-why-a-typical-white -household-has-16-times-the-wealth-of-a-black-one/#48b746d81f45.

Stiglitz, Joseph E. *The Great Divide: Unequal Societies and What We Can Do about Them*. New York: W. W. Norton, 2015.

———. *The Price of Inequality: How Today's Divided Society Endangers Our Future*. New York: W. W. Norton, 2013.

White, Stuart. "Inequality Is Not Our Fate: The Way Back to an Egalitarian Society." *Boston Review*, November 9, 2015. http://bostonreview.net/books-ideas/stuart -white-inequality-atkinson-mason-piketty.

FURTHER INFORMATION

Books

Behnke, Alison Marie. *Racial Profiling: Everyday Inequality*. Minneapolis: Twenty-First Century Books, 2017.

Desmond, Matthew. *Evicted: Poverty and Profit in the American City*. New York: Broadway Books, 2017.

Edge, Laura B. *We Stand as One: The International Ladies Garment Workers Strike, New York, 1909*. Minneapolis: Twenty-First Century Books, 2011.

Edin, Kathryn J., and Luke Shaefer. *$2.00 a Day: Living on Almost Nothing in America*. New York: Mariner Books, 2016.

Ehrenreich, Barbara. *Nickel and Dimed: On (Not) Getting By in America*. New York: Picador, 2011.

Higgins, Nadia Abushanab. *Feminism: Reinventing the F-Word*. Minneapolis: Twenty-First Century Books, 2016.

Jones, Patrick. *Teen Incarceration: From Cell Bars to Ankle Bracelets*. Minneapolis: Twenty-First Century Books, 2017.

MacLeod, Jay. *Ain't No Makin' It: Aspirations and Attainment in a Low-Income Neighborhood*. Boulder, CO: Westview, 2009.

Morris, Charles R. *A Rabble of Dead Money: The Great Crash and the Global Depression: 1929–1939*. New York: PublicAffairs, 2017.

Wilkinson, Richard, and Kate Pickett. *The Spirit Level: Why Greater Equality Makes Societies Stronger*. New York: Bloomsbury, 2010.

Websites

Center for Responsive Politics
http://www.opensecrets.org
The Center for Responsive Politics is a nonpartisan, nonprofit research group that tracks money in US politics and analyzes how it affects elections and public policy.

Inequality.org
http://inequality.org
This website from the Institute for Policy Studies features articles and statistics about economic inequality, along with links to additional resources. It also tells citizens how they can take political action to help reduce economic inequality.

Sunlight Foundation
https://sunlightfoundation.com
The Sunlight Foundation works to make government and politics more accountable to citizens and more transparent—more open and honest about behind-the-scenes practices.

The World's Billionaires
https://www.forbes.com/billionaires/
Hosted by *Forbes*, a business magazine, this website profiles the world's superrich.

Audio

Lutton, Linda. "The View from Room 205: Can Schools Make the American Dream Real for Poor Kids?" *WEBZ91.5Chicago*, January 16, 2017. http://interactive .wbez.org/room205/. This broadcast focuses on fourth graders at a public school in Chicago and how they struggle to succeed in the face of poverty.

NPR staff. "One Restaurant's Recipe for Social Good: Same Meals, Different Prices." *NPR*, August 28, 2016. http://www.npr.org/sections/thesalt/2016/09/02 /492240882/one-restaurants-recipe-for-social-good-same-meals-different-prices. One Los Angeles restaurant chain charges different prices at different locations, depending on whether the neighborhood is rich or poor. In this way, the owners try to provide healthy and delicious food to every customer, regardless of income. At this site, National Public Radio profiles the restaurant.

Vedantam, Shankar. "What's It Like to Be Rich? Ask the People Who Manage Billionaires' Money." *WBAA*, October 25, 2016. http://wbaa.org/post/whats -it-be-rich-ask-people-who-manage-billionaires-money#stream/0. In this segment from National Public Radio, a sociologist shares what she learned by interviewing those who manage the money of the world's wealthiest people. Not surprisingly, the program reveals that the superrich have very different concerns, lifestyles, and attitudes about work and money than most other people.

Video

The Big Short. West Hollywood, CA: Regency Enterprises, 2015. This fictional film shines a spotlight on the housing crisis of the early twenty-first century by weaving together three separate story lines.

Inequality for All. Los Angeles: 72 Productions, 2013. This documentary looks at the economic and political forces responsible for widening inequality in the twenty-first century. The accompanying website, http://inequalityforall.com/, provides more resources and information.

99%: The Occupy Wall Street Collaborative Film. New York: Gigantic Pictures, 2013. The 2011 Occupy Wall Street movement helped awaken American society to the issue of economic inequality. This documentary film tells Occupy's story.

INDEX

ABOUT THE AUTHOR

Coral Celeste Frazer has a master's degree in sociology from Princeton
University and a longstanding interest in issues of inequality, collective
action, and social justice. She writes nonfiction and fiction for teens
and adults, as well as reading comprehension items for the Test of
English as a Foreign Language (TOEFL). She has lived in Colorado,
Oregon, New Jersey, and Boston and now resides in Norwich, England,
with her husband and son.

PHOTO ACKNOWLEDGMENTS

The images in this book are used with the permission of: iStock.com/MicroStockHub
(money); iStock.com/Savushkin (concrete background); iStock.com/Juhku (cracked
background); VCG/VCG/Getty Images, p. 5; M&N/Alamy Stock Photo, p. 7;
en:Puck (magazine); Mayer Merkel & Ottmann lith., N.Y.; Published by Keppler
& Schwarzmann/Wikimedia Commons (Public Domain), p. 9; Ullstein Bild/
Getty Images, p. 12; iStock.com/undercrimson, p. 13; Bettmann/Getty Images,
p. 15; Library of Congress, p. 16; Image courtesy of The Advertising Archives, p. 17;
Bettmann/Getty Images, p. 19; Justine Mathew/Getty Images, p. 21; Jim West/
Alamy Stock Photo, p. 22; iStock.com/fozzyb, p. 25; Rob Nelson/The LIFE Images
Collection/Getty Images, p. 28; © Laura Westlund/Independent Picture Service,
pp. 30, 32, 35, 40, 43; iStock.com/kali9, p. 39; Joe Raedle/Getty Images, p. 48; Mark
Wilson/Getty Images, p. 51; Viviane Moos/Corbis/Getty Images, p. 52; Spencer Platt/
Getty Images, p. 54; Bettmann Archive/Getty Images, p. 57; "Visions of America,
LLC"/Alamy Stock Photo, p. 61; Douglas Graham/Congressional Quarterly/Getty
Images, p. 65; Bill Greene/The Boston Globe/Getty Images, p. 69; REUTERS/
Andrew Burton, p. 71; National Archives, p. 75; Mario Tama/Getty Images,
p. 80;Courtesy Bill Whitford, p. 81; Ivan Couronne/AFP/Getty Images, p. 83; Bill
O'Leary/The Washington Post/Getty Images, p. 87; Jim Watson/AFP/Getty Images,
p. 88; Andrew Burton/Getty Images, p. 91; Courtesy of Michelle Lewis, p. 95; Jim
Cummins/The Image Bank/Getty Images, p. 100; TIM SLOAN/AFP/Getty Images,
p. 102; Chicago Tribune/Tribune News Service/Getty Images, p. 105; Erik Mcgregor/
Pacific Press/LightRocket/Getty Images, p. 109; iStock.com/jacoblund, p. 110;
© John Keatley/Redux, p. 113.

Front and back cover: iStock.com/MicroStockHub (money); iStock.com/Savushkin
(concrete background); iStock.com/Juhku (cracked background).